On Top of Your Game

Kathy,

Your strength,
passion, and perseverance
are inspirational.
Keep feeding
the athlete!

Carrie Moore

On Top of Your Game

Mental Skills to Maximize Your Athletic Performance

Carrie Cheadle

FEED THE ATHLETE PRESS

Published by:

Feed the Athlete Press
P.O. Box 2595
Petaluma, CA 94953
Email: feedtheathlete@gmail.com

Printed in the United States of America

ISBN: 0989691608
ISBN-13: 9780989691604

Library of Congress Control Number: 2013947961
Feed the Athlete Press, Petaluma, CA

For my husband,

> *"To love someone deeply gives you strength.*
> *Being loved by someone deeply gives you courage."*
> — Lao Tzu

I am a stronger, braver person because of you.

TABLE OF CONTENTS

INTRODUCTION

"What do you think ... should we do one more run?"

These were the words spoken to me by my husband in 2002 while we were enjoying the last day of our ski season at Kirkwood Mountain Ski Resort. He's a telemark skier and I'm a snowboarder. We had recently moved away from our home in South Lake Tahoe so I could pursue a master's degree. It was our first year of having to travel to the mountains in order to participate in the snow sports that we loved, which meant we were getting less time on the snow. During each trip to Tahoe, we relished the time we got on the mountain. In hindsight, when my husband asked if I wanted to do one more run, what I should have said to him was...

"No, I'm good. I've had a pretty awesome season and I think I'll just end it there."

What I <u>did</u> say was ...

"Yeah — let's do one more."

At that point I was a year into my graduate program studying sport psychology and despite having less time on the snow, I was having an incredible snowboarding season. I had made some major breakthroughs, largely due to the fact that I was implementing the sport psychology principles and techniques I was learning about. Everything I learned in the classroom I brought with me to the mountain and it was having a profound effect on my performance.

Nobody tears their MCL snowboarding. It's ridiculous. Absurd. It's a skier's injury, not a snowboarder's. Besides, injury was the absolute furthest thing from my mind as my husband and I rode the lift to take the last run of the day on our last day of the season. My husband and I were laughing and talking, and I was reflecting on what a great season it had been for me. As I got off the lift, I caught an edge and my board stopped, but my body kept going. The accident was a total fluke, but it was immediately apparent that I was injured. I was just about to celebrate my best season and instead, I was being lifted onto an emergency sled.

This wasn't my first time dealing with a knee injury. Four years earlier I tore my meniscus and had to have surgery. I was twenty-four years old and it was the first significant injury I'd had. I struggled with not being able to play any of my sports, and I had a really difficult time during my road to recovery. Never had I been more aware of a part of my body. Not just during the physical pain of rehabilitation, but for *months* after. I lived with the fear of whether or not my knee would allow me to participate and perform in my sports the way I had before, and trusting that my knee was strong enough and I wouldn't get re-injured – my body was healed way before my mind ever was. During that snowboarding trip when I injured my knee for the second time, I went through all of the emotions that every athlete goes through when they first get injured; I was confused, scared, angry, and sad, but this time I experienced something else as well. As I took my ride down the mountain in the emergency sled, despite the unbelievable pain I was in and the fact that I knew I was in for a long recovery, I actually felt calm. It seems crazy to me as I write it now, but a part of me was even *excited* to be able to go through this process while I was entrenched in learning about sport psychology. I wasn't even down the mountain yet and I *knew* that this time I was going to come back physically *and* mentally stronger. The confidence I felt in that moment was absolute. There was no doubt, no question in my mind. I knew that my road to recovery would be vastly different than what I had experienced with my previous knee injury. I knew that this time I had the knowledge and tools necessary to be resilient. I knew I could positively face the challenges of my rehabilitation and overcome my fears and anxieties so I could be sure of a comeback the following year. Sure enough, that is exactly what I did. That absolute confidence came to me because I had the knowledge and tools you are about to gain by reading this book.

If you've ever felt nervous getting back into your sport after an injury, performed better in training than in competition, wished you were enjoying your sport more, or felt you've been your own biggest obstacle, reading this book is the first step in taking back control of your performance. Many athletes and coaches say they think competition is 50% physical and 50% mental, but no matter what percentage you put on it, it is undeniable that there is both a physical and mental component involved with sport performance. How often do you practice working on your mental game? How often do you practice your confidence, motivation, and focus? Whether you are an elite athlete performing at the highest levels of your sport, a competitive athlete working your way up the ranks, or an age-grouper challenging yourself to see what you're capable of, *everyone* deserves to feel what it's like; *you* deserve to feel what it's like to be at your best. Part of being your best includes working on the mental aspects of your game.

Competition sets the stage for you to test your ability. It provides you with the context to gauge your improvements and feel immense pride when you overcome challenges and see the fruits of your labor. If you participate in a sport, you have chosen the competitive environment as your stage. The catch, however, is that included in that environment is pressure, stress, anxiety, challenge, struggle, disappointment, fear, anger, and doubt. It is a battle against your competition and a battle against yourself. But... the competitive environment also includes joy, amazement, triumph, pride, courage, and feeling like you are on top of the world. Performing under pressure, dealing with butterflies, and making mistakes are all part of being an athlete. When you feel like you've been knocked down, you have to regain your focus, your drive to do your best, and most of all, your belief that you will once again perform to your potential. In short: you've got to fall in love again with your sport, and the information and tools provided in this book help you do just that.

The work you do on your mental game is just as important as all of the other factors that impact your performance. *On Top of Your Game* provides exercises to inspire you and lead you to overcome your fears and get you back to performing to your potential. You can read through the book in its entirety and build a complete foundation for your mental game, and you can also use it as a continued resource throughout your athletic life. Throughout different seasons you may find that you need to focus on a specific area and you can turn right to the chapter that addresses that topic. If you're feeling some burnout, you can go straight to Chapter Two and read about motivation. If you have moments when you feel plagued with negative thoughts and doubts, you can turn to Chapter Five and read about how to relax your mind and harness the power of your thoughts so they positively affect your performance. If you've encountered a setback during your season, you can go to Chapter Nine and remind yourself of how to turn obstacles into opportunities.

Every chapter in this book takes you on a journey through a specific topic that has a significant impact on whether you feel anxiety and doubt or feel resilient and confident when it comes to your sport. As you absorb this knowledge and implement the tools, you will be building a solid foundation of mental skills and mental toughness. You will be provided with the exact tools I have used with hundreds of athletes to help them overcome their own performance anxieties and perform to their potential. In each chapter you will be introduced to ideas and techniques that will help you master your mental game and take charge of your athletic performance. I've changed some of the specific details regarding individual athletes, but every story and anecdote is true. The end of each chapter highlights five main messages and walks you step-by-step through two Mental Skills Training tools that you can immediately implement into your own mental game plan. Each tool has been designed to help boost your confidence and help you effectively deal with the challenges that come with being an athlete. In addition to the applied exercises and tools provided in the book, there are supplemental resources available to you online. Every tool in this book can be accessed as an actual worksheet at www.carriecheadle.com.

This is a hands-on book. If you really want to improve your mental game — strengthen your mental fitness — you need to decide it's a priority and then dedicate the time to work on it. What you are about to read is what you need in order to perform more consistently, build more confidence, and have more control over your performance — *if you do the work*. If you want to believe in your ability to accomplish your goals, achieve more consistent results, and stop yourself from being your own biggest obstacle, let this book coach you and be your guide to staying on top of your game.

Throughout my work as a Mental Skills Coach, I have had many athletes come to me because they are experiencing performance anxiety. These athletes put an unbearable amount of pressure on themselves to perform, which inevitably created the physical and psychological tension that ultimately sabotaged their performances. I wrote this book because I saw athletes losing hope. I saw athletes that had tremendous passion and motivation, but found themselves starting to wonder if they should continue competing. They wanted to compete, but were frustrated knowing that they weren't performing to their potential. They knew that somehow they were getting in their own way, but didn't know how not to. They felt like their brains and bodies had been hijacked by anxiety and they were desperate to do something about it.

I wrote this book for *you*. I wanted you to know that you don't have to suffer, that there is another way. I wanted you to know that you don't have to struggle anymore, that you can regain your passion for your sport, stop holding yourself back from performing your best, and have fun again. As a Mental Skills Coach with over ten years of experience working with everyone from the first time triathlete to Olympians, I counsel athletes every day on how to regain not only their physical prowess, but more importantly, their confidence in themselves. If you are reading this book, it means that you know you have more potential. I know you have more potential too. When you dedicate yourself to your sport, you deserve to get the most out of that experience, perform to your potential, and be on top of your game.

—*Carrie*

chapter 1

PERFORMING UNDER PRESSURE

"What's bigger than butterflies? A buzzard?
I had a buzzard in my stomach."
—Allen Iverson, professional basketball player

E very book ever written on the topic of anxiety and sport performance starts out with a story about an inspirational athlete that rises to the occasion when it counts, when their team needs them the most. The clock is ticking, the winning point is on the line, *the pressure is on*, and it all comes down to one moment. But what about the athlete that feels pressure before they even step onto the field? This could be the middle-aged mom or dad training hard for their first marathon; the star college hurdler coming back to compete in the first meet after an injury; the high school varsity baseball player that knows there are college scouts watching in the stands. For these athletes, some professional, but many like you or me, dedicated to a sport they have come to love — what if the same pressure to perform has now developed into debilitating performance anxiety? What if that athlete is plagued with worries and doubts, not just the morning before competition, but for *days* before?

This type of performance anxiety causes you to trigger your fight-or-flight response which results in physiological symptoms than can have a negative effect on your performance. Your heart beats faster, your stomach is in knots, your reaction time slows down, and you are competing well below your capability. These athletes often make the decision to come to me as a last ditch effort to save their athletic career.

> *During my last game there were college coaches watching from the stands and I knew that I had to perform well. I want to play in college so badly that every time the college coaches come to watch I put so much pressure on myself that I play horribly. I know it's my head that gets in my way. It's like I'm not even the same player when they come to watch.*

> *Ever since I crashed in that bike race I feel like I haven't been the same. Every descent I am slower and I ride tentative and unsure. If it's steep and technical or there are other riders around, then forget it. I used to be the fastest descender on my team; it was my strength. Now it's the descents that are holding me back and I don't even want to show up to race. All I think about is crashing. If I can't get my head back in it, I'm done.*

Many of the athletes I have worked with over the years have come to me to help them "get over" their performance anxiety. These athletes have begun to lose hope. They think to themselves, "I just get nervous. I can't control it and there is nothing I can do about it." After a particularly debilitating episode — freezing up at the plate, unable to get back on their bikes after a bruising fall — they are left with a sense that this world has been closed to them.

Sport is our battleground. It's the place we go to see what we're made of. The emotions we experience during a game or competition when absolutely everything comes together is unlike any other feeling in the world. The hours of practice you put in just paid off. You made all the right decisions and you were unstoppable. The penalty kick was perfectly placed in the net and there was nothing that the goalie could do to stop it, you sank the putt you needed in order to beat your opponent, you got the holeshot and stayed out front the entire race. That's the feeling that keeps you coming back, the feeling of coming out on top. However, performing under pressure is a part of that package. As an athlete, if you internalize that pressure, things can start to get miserable — and your performance suffers. Butterflies will be a part of your journey; if competition were a walk in the park, your triumphs wouldn't mean anything. Performing under pressure is part of the culture of sport. However, if the butterflies you feel are so overwhelming that you're thinking about quitting your sport, it's beyond time to do something about it.

As a Mental Skills Coach with over ten years of experience working with everyone from the first time triathlete, the Olympic hopeful, to the professional athlete, I counsel athletes everyday on how to regain not only their physical prowess, but more importantly, their confidence in themselves. I have worked with many athletes that have gone through the torture of debilitating nerves before an event. At times it can feel insurmountable, the adrenaline, the doubting of yourself after countless hours of practice. No one should feel like they have to give up their sport when they are still physically healthy, still have the desire to participate, and still feel tremendous passion for their sport.

Stress is an integral part of the human condition. From daily life stressors, to huge life events, everyone has experienced some form of stress. For some people, even saying the words "stress" or "anxiety" will evoke feelings of nervousness and tension. At the mere mention of the words, you may realize you are holding your breath and feel a tightening in your chest. This is just at the *thought* of being nervous. Get yourself into an actual pressure-filled situation and the symptoms are even more intense. Athletes are constantly faced with situations in which they must perform under pressure. Right before a race, in the pool, on the track, in the ring, an athlete's ability to deal with stress and its possible effects on performance is an important topic for athletes, coaches, and people like me who are working with athletes on their mental game. If you are reading this book, chances are that at some point in your athletic endeavors you have felt some version of sweaty palms and a racing heart while competing in your sport. And while some healthy nervousness is useful if channeled correctly, the goal of this book is to give you the tools you need to get you to the start line feeling confident, focused, and in control, and to use your nerves to help power you forward, not drag you down.

What Exactly Are We Dealing With?

Stress, fear, and anxiety are terms we tend to use interchangeably. Whatever label you choose, it is typically experienced as something unpleasant. There's a good reason why you can just "fill-in-the-blank" with any of these terms; they are very closely connected to one another. However, there are important differences between the three.

The word *stress* can take on many different meanings so it is important to explain exactly what we are dealing with. People typically use the word stress to describe either the emotion they feel or the pressure they are under; "I'm feeling stressed" or "I'm under a lot of stress". As an athlete, you can experience feeling "stressed" when you are faced with some sort of demand and there is a need for you to respond to that demand; the demand you need to respond to is the *stressor*; the event causing the stress. Getting in a four-hour training ride, shooting a free throw, healing from an injury, playing in a championship game; these are all stressors that an athlete might face. A stressor can originate physiologically or psychologically, meaning the demand can be something that originates in your body, or the demand can be something that originates in your mind. Even though these things can bring you joy and a sense of accomplishment as an athlete, they can also cause this feeling of stress when called on to perform.

Examples of *physiological stressors* are:

- Getting injured
- Increase in training load
- Extreme changes in temperature
- Fighting off an infection
- Malnutrition
- Overtraining
- Surgery
- Lack of sleep

Examples of potential *psychological stressors* are:

- You approach the start line and look around at the competition
- You miss a routine play
- Your team is behind in the score

You may have noticed that I used the word *potential* psychological stressors. The situations above aren't *actual* stressors; they are common occurrences that come up in competition. *Your perception of the situation and your assessment of your ability to handle yourself in that situation will determine whether you characterize them as "stressful" or not.* Those are just situations; *these* are stressors:

- You approach the start line and look around. You start sizing up the competition and make judgments about whether or not you fit in. Now you are calculating your chances of success (or chances of failure) based on who you see around you.

- You miss a routine play. You berate yourself for making such a stupid error. Now you're consumed with anxious thoughts of making another error and you can't turn it off. To make things worse you add to your stress by constantly glancing at the bench, just waiting for your coach to pull you from the game.

- You are chosen to be the lead rider for an upcoming race. You feel a tremendous amount of pressure to perform for your team. You're afraid you won't be able to pull out the win and you'd much rather just ride for someone else on the team.

The reasons these situations have become stressors is because the athlete perceived them to be a threat. When there is a discrepancy between a demand and your perception of whether or not you feel you can meet that demand, you feel stress.

Whether the stressor is initiated in the body or in the mind, they both lead to a physiological response. You have assessed that there is something to be stressed about and the emotions associated with stress will coincide with biochemical changes in your body that prepare you to deal with the threatening situation. This is your *stress-response*. It is the physiological response in the body that prepares you to be able to run or to fight when faced with a threatening situation, also known as your "fight-or-flight" response. The intensity of this response will be different depending on the person and the situation. For some people, the thought of sleeping on a portaledge (basically a hanging cot) 1000 feet above the valley floor while climbing El Capitan in Yosemite National Park sends waves of terror throughout their body. For others, sleeping on a portaledge is no problem, but when they imagine singing solo in front of an audience of 1000, they also imagine running out the backstage door. Whether it's beneficial or detrimental to the immediate situation, your body has already responded in the way it is designed to respond to the perception of a threat.

Fear and anxiety are emotions that alert you to some sort of danger. They are emotions that you may experience when faced with a stressor. *Fear* alerts you to an immediate threat and *anxiety* involves concerns about the potential of a future threat. Anxiety is worry, fear is real. With the emotion of fear, the danger is real and immediate. We feel the emotion so we will respond to the threat. If you see a line drive coming at your head, your fear gets you to catch the ball or get out of the way. Anxiety is an emotion caused by the *thought* of a possible threat. Like fear, anxiety is also designed to get us to act. If the emotion of anxiety has done its job then it has mobilized you to prepare for a potential future threat. However, anxiety can either cause you to avoid, over-prepare, or adequately prepare for the situation. You don't want to get hit in the face with a line drive so you can *avoid* (never put yourself into a situation where a line drive will be coming at you) *over-prepare* (carry a glove and wear a face mask and helmet 24 hours/day so you will be protected if ever a line drive should be coming at you) or *prepare* (learn and practice catching line drives). In some situations, anxiety can even cause you to *under-prepare* so you have a built-in excuse if things don't go well. The problem is that you can trigger your stress-response when the situation is *perceived* as a threat and not an *actual* threat. Situations aren't stressors; *it is the athlete's perception that they can't handle the situation that is the stressor.* When you feel like you cannot cope with the demand you will feel the emotions of fear or anxiety.

The effects of psychological stress depend on how the demand is interpreted. Two different people can be met with the same challenge, but their individual interpretation of the situation will predict how they respond. Here are some examples of how two different athletes can interpret the same situation in two different ways:

Situation: The team lost the last four games and is about to play an undefeated team.

Athlete A: Checks out the competition during the warm-up and already feels defeated before the game starts.
Athlete B: Focuses on getting mentally and physically prepared and imagines how good it will feel to make this the game that turns around their losing streak.

Situation: The athlete about to enter the first game after an ACL injury.

Athlete A: Is plagued with visions of reinjuring her knee and is hoping that the coach decides to play someone else.
Athlete B: Knows she did all of her rehabilitation and trusts that her body is ready to handle competition.

Situation: The athlete shows up to the venue to prepare for an event and forgot an essential piece of equipment.

Athlete A: Immediately panics and feels like he just blew the whole race. He isn't motivated to figure out Plan B because he feels like he has already lost.

Athlete B: Has already gone into Plan B mode. He immediately thinks, "It doesn't matter what equipment I use. I'm ready and I'm here to do this," and then he goes down his mental checklist of how to borrow or obtain the gear he needs.

Two athletes enter; one athlete succeeds. Whether something transforms into anxiety has to do with your *perception* of the situation. When you feel like you cannot cope with the demand, the thought of the stressor (and the consequences) manifest into feelings of anxiety. The *anticipation* of something that *might* happen now becomes the stressor. If you feel like there are times when you have a tendency to be more like Athlete A, this book will give you the tools to have more experiences like Athlete B.

Why Do We Get Anxious?

When I was in high school, I was *notorious* for worrying the night before an exam. Despite my hours of studying, I was always afraid that I was going to fail the test (and to me "failing" meant getting an A-... or worse a B!). Test after test I would prove myself wrong by getting a good grade, but inevitably as the next exam approached, I would repeat the same exact cycle. My mother used to repeatedly say to me, "I don't know why you worry so much, you always get a good grade!" Why wasn't each previous good grade proof enough to alleviate my future anxiety?

People tend to be bad at calculating the actual possibility of an unfavorable outcome and the odds in your mind tend to lean more towards disaster than triumph. If you fall more towards the "stressed" side versus the "carefree" side of the continuum, then you're more likely to anticipate failure than you are to anticipate success. There are as many sources of anxiety as there are athletes. As athletes, we tend to experience the most anxiety when we are faced with the following situations:

The outcome is important to you

You know that there are scouts in the stands and you feel like this is your one big opportunity for them to see how you play. It's the championship game, the winning point is on the line, and you feel like the entire outcome of the game is up to you (think penalty kick, field goal, 3-pointer, etc.). Many times, the fact that you're nervous is a good indicator that this is something important to you; the outcome of the event is meaningful to you. In this scenario, athletes can put additional pressure on themselves because of the importance of the outcome. It's an awful feeling to walk away from a performance *knowing* you could have done better and that your nerves got in your way.

The situation is new and you don't know what to expect

We tend to experience those dreaded "what-ifs" in novel situations. Here are a couple examples:
You are racing on a new course and won't have a chance to check out the venue before your event:

- ***What if*** *the course is harder than I thought?"*
- ***What if*** *it isn't well-marked and I get off course?"*

You are switching teams and/or coaches and are concerned with whether or not it will be a good fit for you:

- *"**What if** I don't like my teammates and coaches?"*
- *"**What if** they don't like me?"*
- *"**What if** we disagree on training and technique?"*

New situations are prime time for you to worry about things that *might* happen. (We'll get back to those dreaded "what-ifs" in Chapter Five when we talk about how to relax your mind.)

Things are unpredictable

You can experience feelings of stress when things are unpredictable: You are doing the same training program and you aren't achieving the same results. Your coach seems to have no rhyme or reason for choosing who starts in the game. Lack of consistency and not knowing what to expect is stressful. There is great comfort in knowing and trusting that if you do "A" the consequence is "B". It's a little more stressful if the outcome is more unpredictable and doesn't seem to have any kind of pattern to it. If you do "A" the consequence could be A, B, C, F, H, M, Z, 12, 17, or 23!

You feel like you have no control

You can experience feelings of stress in situations when you perceive you have no control. There is nothing you can do about the situation you are in: Your coach is telling you to make changes in your technique or your training program. The other team is pushing the pace of the game and you don't know if you can keep up. You want to get to the competition venue at a certain time, but are stuck in a situation where you have no control over what time you actually arrive. It can be extremely anxiety provoking when you want something to be different and you feel like you have no control to change it.

Fear of failure

Participating in sport can become a threat to your ego when you assign too much meaning to the outcome of an event. You wonder "What will people think of me if ..." You have internalized both the real and perceived external pressures that you feel. More often than not, *you* are the person putting the most pressure on yourself. Fear of losing or making mistakes can cause tremendous anxiety and be extremely detrimental to your performance. A great example of this is when cyclists hold back from putting in an all out effort during a race because they're afraid that if they go too hard, they won't have enough for the final sprint. These cyclists can go through their entire careers never knowing exactly how much effort they can put out because their fear of failing causes them to always hold a little bit back. They will never know what was possible for them because they were too afraid to take the risk and finished every race feeling like they could have pushed harder.

You are experiencing life stress

Anxiety begets anxiety. When you are experiencing other stressors in your life they can inevitably bleed into your athletic life as well. In his brilliant book *Why Zebras Don't Get Ulcers: The Acclaimed Guide to Stress, Stress-Related Disease, and Coping*, author Robert M. Sapolsky explains that if you are faced with a sudden stressor and you have already been stressed, your response to that stressor is going to be more intense.

Dealing with life stressors like issues at school, home, or work means that by the time game day comes your cup is already full. Managing life stress can provide you with more room in your cup to deal with the stressors of training and competition.

———

There are numerous reasons why athletes become nervous before competition. Chances are you have worries and doubts that fit into more than one category. One of the first exercises in this book helps you give a voice to some of those anxieties and figure out which categories they fall into. Now that we have defined some terms and you have an understanding of why athletes get anxious, it's time to explore the physiological impact of your stress-response.

How the Body and Brain Work

Your body is constantly trying to achieve equilibrium. There is an ideal state for everything and your body is always working to get back to that ideal state. A great example of this is body temperature. Your body likes to be somewhere around 97°–99°F. If you head outside and it's 30°F, your body conserves heat by restricting blood vessels to reduce heat loss. If you need to generate more heat, you will start to shiver. Go back inside where someone has cranked up the thermostat and your body dilates your blood vessels to get rid of some heat. If you are still too hot, your body will sweat to help you cool off and get your temperature back to normal. Earlier I mentioned that the stress-response involves biochemical changes in the body to prepare you to deal with an immediate or potential threat. All of those changes happen in your *nervous system*. Basically, the role of your nervous system is to receive, process, and respond to information. Your nervous system is broken up into different divisions and each division has different responsibilities. We are only going to look at two of those divisions, *sympathetic* and *parasympathetic*.

The *sympathetic division* is in charge of the stress-response. This division is concerned with getting the body ready for "peak performance" in response to a threat. It prepares the body for action. When you stimulate your stress-response, your body releases fast acting hormones that will increase your heart rate, circulation, and oxygen to prepare your body for immediate and superior action. Your body will respond this way whether there is an actual threat, or a perceived threat. Whether an athlete swerves on his bike to avoid a crash or an athlete starts to panic when she is in possession of the ball — each separate scenario leads to the same physiological response.

Whereas the sympathetic division gets you pumped up for action, the *parasympathetic division* has a more calming effect on the body. You can think of it as your *relaxation response*; it cools you off and calms you down. The parasympathetic division is concerned with slowing down the body, having the opposite effect in comparison with the sympathetic division. This division is concerned with daily functioning like what is coming in (digestion) and what is going out (no explanation necessary), promoting growth and energy storage, slowing down your heart rate, and other important things that get thrown out the window when you're under stress. The two divisions work together like a teeter-totter. One division isn't "off" while the other one is "on", instead your body is constantly shifting between both, continually trying to balance each other out and bring you back to "normal".

As you have probably already guessed, your brain plays an important role in all of this. Without getting submerged in the anatomy of the brain, here's what you need to know:

Deep in the middle of your brain there is a little almond shaped structure; this is your amygdala. The amygdala is the part of your brain in charge of emotional memories and emotional meaning. Say you are a cyclist and you roll up to the start line and see some big name cyclist sitting on the line. Your brain starts scanning its memory banks to glean some information about how you should feel and respond to the current situation. Your brain starts processing that information before you even know you're processing it. In the front of your brain, your frontal lobes are in charge of assessing, planning, and intention. When you think about rolling up to the line and start to anticipate who else will be there, your frontal lobes are in control. Frontal lobes interpret signals from the body and assess "Hey, we're stressed" or "Hey, we're cool".

For the cyclist at the starting line, the amygdala is like the first responder on the scene. First responders are trained in advanced first aid and can assist in an emergency until advanced medical assistance becomes available. It starts to assess: "What's happened in this situation before? How did we react?" and this is all happening before your rational mind can override it and decide "Hey man, chill out. Different day, different race, different situation. No hay problema amygdala, we got this." If the amygdala detects a threat, it can immediately activate the stress-response to prepare to address the threat. If you've had prior experiences getting nervous before a race, the amygdala has already put things in motion before you have decided whether or not you're nervous. It picks up on cues and compares it to the storage of emotional memories. It opens the photo album marked "racing" and sees images of you rolling up to the line feeling nervous and then it says to the body "Yep — sound the alarm. It's time to freak out. Mobilize the stress-response, stat." The more rational parts of your brain can come in and override the amygdala. They can take over from the first responder and say "We got it from here," and then reassess the situation with the additional information and knowledge they have.

However, the rational mind isn't always rational. The frontal lobes can spin tales of dreaded "what-ifs"... your thoughts can feed into the situation and create a stressor. If you're overly anxious, you'll see threats where other people won't. Remember the differences between Athlete A and Athlete B? Athlete A is nervous before he even rolls up to the start. As he rolls up the amygdala is assessing "Yep — we have definitely been nervous in this situation before — prepare to be nervous." Athlete A may have even checked out the start list the night before the race to see who was showing up, which means that his "rational" mind was already "rationalizing" why he should be nervous. You can see how stress can become a vicious negative feedback loop. Both the amygdala and the frontal lobes can play a role in strengthening the activation of the stress-response. Anxiety causes alarm in the body and alarm in the body causes anxiety.

The frontal lobes can create negative thoughts and worries that manifest into stressors that trigger the stress-response. But those same frontal lobes can also override the stress-response. If Athlete B checks out the start list to see who is showing up, it is so he will be prepared for the strengths and capitalize on the weaknesses of his opponents, not to psych himself out before the race even starts. Your brain is basically what activates your stress-response, but if you have a history of activating that stress-response in certain situations, the brain picks up on those cues and automatically starts that response before the thought "I'm nervous" even enters your mind. That neural pathway gets strengthened even further when you then expect to be nervous going into future events. What's amazing is that you can start to cool off your stress-response once you *decide* that there is no threat. *YOU* can help yourself get back to homeostasis. If you are a skier looking down the slope of an advanced run and feel like you are about to get in above your head, your stress-response will be activated. If you can look down that slope and think to yourself, "I can do this. I can traverse and go at my own speed; this is within my ability," your heart stars to slow down and your shoulders relax because you've changed your perception of the threat.

How Does Anxiety Impact Performance?

How do you know when you are nervous? If you think back to the last time you were feeling some performance anxiety, you can probably list the physical symptoms you experienced:

- Your heart is racing and/or feels like it's going to burst out of your chest.
- You have a slightly unsettled or nauseous feeling in your stomach, also known as butterflies.
- Your thoughts are moving faster than usual.
- You've wiped your sweaty hands on your shirt three times in that last two minutes.
- Your breathing has become shallow or you even find yourself holding your breath.
- Your cheeks and neck look like they've been sunburned.
- Your shoulders are tense (and your hands, neck, face, jaw, etc.).
- You feel shaky and jittery and it's not because of your pre-game shot of espresso.

- You've gone to the bathroom twice already and are wondering if you need to go again before the game or race starts.

OK, *your* actual list may look a little different than this one. Whenever I ask participants this question in a workshop, there are always some common symptoms and some that are unique to each athlete. If you don't enjoy the symptoms you feel they can make you miserable. Not only do you often interpret the physiological symptoms of your anxiety as unpleasant, but there are also some other darn good reasons to get your anxiety under control. Here are some additional effects that anxiety (and eliciting your stress response) can have on your performance:

- Increased muscular tension
- Increased fatigue
- Tunnel vision
- Decreased balance and coordination
- Increased distractibility
- Decreased ability to make decisions
- Increased likelihood of injury
- Decreased growth and tissue repair
- Decreased immune system
- Interferes with amount and quality of sleep

Not only can these factors impact your performance, but they can impact your recovery from training and competition as well. The above list might as well be titled, "Things That Will Keep You from Ever Performing to Your Potential". If you have been putting off working on this part of your game, your time has come. Working on your mental game will not only help you feel less miserable, but it will have a real impact on your physical performance.

Anxiety Gets a Bad Rap

Anxiety isn't all bad. Getting nervous before competition is normal. In fact, some athletes report that they would feel "off" if they didn't experience some nerves before competition. When you experience the physiological symptoms of anxiety and then label those symptoms as "bad" — that will contribute to the unease that you feel. We tend to put the stamp of "bad" or "good" onto many situations and emotions. The label you choose to assign to the situation or emotion will depict your response to that situation. The fact that many of us deem the *feeling* of anxiety as "bad" exacerbates how uncomfortable it actually feels.

Anxiety is hard-wired in us for a reason. It serves an important purpose in our lives. Anxiety is an emotion that we feel to encourage us to deal with a situation we are being presented with. Anxiety arises from fear and is meant to propel us to create solutions to deal with an emerging threat. However, sometimes you can get stuck in that cycle of worry and the feelings of anxiety can become overwhelming and detrimental to your performance. The doubts and worries that can accompany anxiety can become a vicious negative feedback loop, reinforcing the anxiety you feel until you do something to stop the cycle. The problem is that most athletes don't know what to do to get control of their anxiety and start enjoying their sport again.

This chapter has introduced you to what is going on when your nerves have taken over and your performance suffers. The rest of the book tells you what to do about it. If you picked up this book wondering if you will ever be able to enjoy your sport again – the answer is YES! Wishing things would change is not going to make anything different. If you want to feel more confident and in control of your performance, then you are going to have to work for it and working for it starts right now. Don't just read the chapters – do the work at the end of each chapter. (Your first assignment is to create your own mental skills training binder so you have a place to collect all of your worksheets and reflections in one place!) If you aren't willing to work then you might as well pass this book on to someone else. Your athletic journey may have started years ago, but you are about to embark down a new road. The goal isn't to get rid of your anxiety, but to give you the tools to manage it.

Chapter 1: Take-Aways

- It's normal to feel nervous before competition. Performing under pressure is part of the culture of sport. However, if your nerves are affecting your performance it's time to do something about it.
- You can create stressors in your mind when you perceive that you can't meet a demand. You can also create stressors when you are afraid of something that might happen in the future. You brain can exacerbate or alleviate your stress-response.
- Anxiety isn't bad. Anxiety is an emotion you feel that is designed to get you to act, to prepare for upcoming competitions. When you put a "bad" stamp on anxiety it makes the situation feel worse.
- The goal isn't to erase your anxiety. Not only is that unrealistic, but it can actually be detrimental to your performance. The goal is to give you the tools to manage it. If you don't learn how to manage your anxiety, you will never perform to your potential.
- You can be Athlete B!

Chapter 1: Tools

Tool: Weight of the World

When you are anxious, you can become so consumed with the physical symptoms of your anxiety and so distracted by your worry and doubts that you don't know exactly what you are anxious about. The first step in breaking this cycle of pre-performance anxiety is to figure out exactly what is causing you to feel stress. Just verbalizing what you are nervous about can help relieve some of that anxiety. Follow the steps below to figure what kind of pressure you are carrying around on your shoulders and how to let some of it go.

TIP: Complete each step before you move on and read the next step. Remember that you can also go to www.carriecheadle.com to get access to free worksheets for each chapter!

Step 1: Draw a little stick figure picture of yourself at the bottom of a piece of paper. Even better, copy and paste an actual picture of yourself! (Now go and do it before you go on and read Step 2).

Step 2: *Go back and do Step 1*. Now, above the picture, write out all of the pressure you have on your shoulders. What is making you nervous about your upcoming competition? Write them in little phrases above your picture.

Step 3: Assign a weight to each item that you wrote. On a scale from 0–100 pounds, how much does each item weigh? The issues that concern you the most will weigh more than the issues that aren't bothering you all that much. Write the weight next to each item.

Step 4: Add together all of the weight. Did your jaw drop? Don't just guess, actually add it all up. Now imagine that you are _literally_ carrying all of that weight on your shoulders as you head into competition; what would happen? (I'm going to go out on a limb and say that if you are a swimmer, you'll be sinking to the bottom of the pool.)

Step 5: Grab a new sheet of paper and create three columns. Pick the bottom three and the top three items from your list and write them in the first column. Write down the weight of each next to the item.

Step 6: For each item, figure out which category it falls into from earlier in the chapter (outcome is important, situation is new, things are unpredictable, you feel like you have no control, fear of failure, life stress). Some items may fall into more than one category so just try to pick the best fit. Write the category next to the item in the second column. This will help you to recognize if there is a pattern of items falling into certain categories.

Step 7: For each item, figure out what would need to be different for you to shave some weight off that item. What could you do to shave off 5 or 10 pounds? Or if that feels like too much, how about one pound? How can you make that item weigh less than it does right now? Start with the items that weigh less until you figure out a strategy for each one. Be as specific as possible and write your strategy in the third column.

Step 8: How much does each item weigh now? Recalculate how much each item weighs after you have shaved off some weight. Add it up to see how much total weight you have shaved off. Do you feel a little bit lighter? If you found this exercise helpful you can continue to do this with the rest of the items on your list. Remember that the goal isn't to eliminate all of the weight but to just relieve some of the pressure you are carrying into your performance. This exercise also helps remind you that YOU have the tools to help shave off the weight — I didn't tell you how to shave it off — you did that yourself. Nice work!

Tool: Peak Performance Vision

It's time to turn back the clock and return to your best performance. The first part of this is a free-writing exercise where you will write about a peak performance you had. In the second part you will answer some questions related to that day.

Step 1: Grab a piece of paper and think back to one of your best performances. First, write out a vivid description of your performance that day. Be descriptive; really bring that day back to life. A great tip for creating powerful images is to incorporate your senses into your description. What kinds of things did you *see* when you arrived to the venue? What *smells* bring that memory back into your mind? What *sounds* did you hear on that day? Write down any memories you have of that day. If you're more artistically inclined, draw a picture of yourself that captures that moment.

Step 2: Now that you have that vision in your mind, take some time to describe how you were feeling (How was your body feeling? How were you feeling emotionally?) and what you were thinking during each phase of your performance. On a second piece of paper:

1. Describe your thoughts and feelings before your performance.
2. Describe your thoughts and feelings during your performance.

3. Describe your thoughts and feelings after your performance.

Step 3: This exercise can help provide you with some self-awareness of the factors involved when you perform your best. When you are nervous going into competition it's difficult to remember that there was ever a time when you were performing well and enjoying your sport. This vision also serves as your reminder of the athlete *you are*. Now that you have it written down, you can read through your Peak Performance Vision and envelop yourself with that image and that feeling of when you were at your best. Pull it out and look it over before practice or competition and remind yourself of how amazing and confident you felt on that day and bring that energy with you into your next practice or event. If that was you then, it can also be you now.

chapter 2

YOUR INNER DRIVE

*"Passion is a huge prerequisite to winning. It makes you willing
to jump through hoops, go through all the ups and downs
and everything in between to reach your goal."*
—Kerri Walsh, Olympic Gold Medalist, beach volleyball

My husband is afraid of heights. Even knowing this fact about him, I always knew that he would love rock climbing. We both loved the mountains and loved outdoor sports. We went snowboarding, hiking, backpacking, white water rafting ... but never rock climbing. I had climbed a few times with friends and I knew my husband (then boyfriend) would love it, but his fear of heights literally grounded him. Fast-forward a few years from that point and we finally added rock climbing to our list of outdoor adventures. There were a few things that contributed to him being able to work through his once debilitating fear of heights. Once he finally climbed, he realized that it was nowhere near as scary as he thought it would be. He removed some of his fear by embracing the philosophy that every challenge he undertook was by his choice. He built up his confidence and courage by recognizing that he had control over his choice of how far to go. Not only did we add it to the list, but we soon revolved our lives around climbing. We went on regular week-long climbing trips to Joshua Tree National Park. We traveled across the country on road trips hitting all the favored climbing spots along the way. I finally got him to climb and we both fell in love with it; he went from refusing to climb, to leading multi-pitch routes. Then a strange thing happened. After a while, any time he would suggest a day of climbing, I immediately didn't want to go. I hemmed and hawed and tried to talk my way out of it and then finally gave up and just forced myself to go.

Chad: "Let's go climb tomorrow."
Carrie: "Yeah, maybe. That might be cool."
Chad: "We can go to Buck Rock."
Carrie: "I don't know; there are a few other things I need to do tomorrow."
Chad: "We can go early and then you can still have time to get stuff done."
Carrie: "It might be crowded tomorrow."
Chad: "Why are you making this so hard!?"
Carrie: "Alright, fine, let's go climb tomorrow."

At the time, I couldn't understand what was happening. I *loved* climbing. I loved being outside. I loved being on the rock and thinking about nothing else but my next move. I loved improving my climbing skills and being able to climb harder routes. It was frustrating for him, and confusing for me; why was I suddenly completely unmotivated to go? I loved to climb, but more often than not, when my husband said "Hey, let's go climbing this weekend" I lost all motivation to go.

It took me a long time to finally realize that I felt I had lost control over my own motivation to climb. Every time my husband suggested a climbing trip I *perceived* I was being forced to go, that the decision was completely out of my hands and I had no control. Chad found his motivation to climb when he realized it was always his choice and I lost my motivation when I thought it was no longer my choice. I needed to remind myself of my own love of climbing and recognize that *I was choosing to climb too*, not being forced to go because he was initiating the trip. Even though it wasn't true, I felt like I had no control and it greatly affected my motivation. Once I realized it, I was able to re-connect with my inner drive and re-discover my love of climbing. As life moved on we became interested in other things and climbing was moved to the back burner to make room for our new goals and interests. Now, fast forward several more years to the present date and as I write this sentence, it's been years since either one of us have climbed. Something we once revolved our lives around is no longer a part of our lives.

―――――――

Motivation is a part of your daily life. You're motivated to eat when you feel hungry, you're motivated to sleep when you feel tired, you're motivated to work so you can pay your bills...motivation influences us every day. As my story demonstrates, motivation can be complicated and can change over time. I wanted to climb and my husband didn't want to climb. Then we both loved to climb and went climbing all the time. Then my husband wanted to climb and I didn't want to climb. Now both of us talk about climbing, but neither of us climb. Motivation is complex because there are many factors that can influence your motivation and your motivation can naturally change over time. Not only can your own motivation change, but what motivates one person might be different than what motivates another. One athlete plays soccer because all of her older siblings played soccer and she is just next in line. Another athlete plays soccer because it's *who he is* — he can't even envision himself without a soccer ball in the picture. One triathlete races because having a race to train for is incentive to get in his workouts. Another triathlete races because she loves the culture, enjoys identifying herself as a triathlete, and loves the way it feels to shave minutes off her time. Most athletes have *multiple* motivational factors that compel them to participate in their sport. Before we get into topics like focus, relaxation techniques, and self-talk — we need to address the topic that supports it all — motivation.

Motivation affects every part of your performance. When you're feeling unmotivated it can affect everything from training to competition. When your level of motivation is low it can:

- Affect your desire to train, which results in making you less prepared for competition
- Be a strain on your relationships making it difficult to communicate with your coaches and teammates
- Knock you off course, derailing you from your goals and causing your performance to stagnate
- Make you feel like you can't handle the obstacles you encounter
- Cause you to barely have enough energy to go through the motions in practice and competition let alone perform to your potential
- Stunt your creativity causing you to be unable to adapt to changes and miss big opportunities
- Affect how you feel about yourself as an athlete
- Affect your enjoyment of your sport

In the world of sport psychology, motivation refers to the direction and intensity of effort. Motivation drives your behavior; it compels you to act because you either want something or you don't want something. You don't want to get hit by a car crossing the street, so you are motivated to walk up to the light and use the crosswalk. You want to get good grades so you can get into the college of your choice, so you are motivated to show up to class and do your homework. You want to do well in competition, so you are motivated to go to practice and stick to your training plan.

In sport, athletes constantly get the romanticized message that if they have enough love for the game, they can overcome anything. Motivation is often oversimplified into terms like *passion* and *heart,* when in fact there are many factors that contribute to an athlete's level of motivation. There will be times when you are extremely motivated to train and compete and times when it will be the last thing you want to do. Your motivation will fluctuate throughout one season, let alone over your entire athletic career. Having times of low motivation is normal, but you want to figure out what's going on because even though it's normal, it's a sign that you should pay attention to.

Internal Versus External Motivation

Many things influence which direction you focus your efforts in, and how much effort you put in. There are two *sources* that underlie motivation and three factors that influence motivation. I'll address the *factors* in a minute — right now we're going to focus on the sources. The two sources of motivation are internal and external. *Internal motivation* is the desire that comes from inside of you. *External motivation* is the motivation that originates outside of you. Internal motivation is your inner drive. This is where your love and passion for your sport comes from. This is what causes your eyes to light up when I ask you what you love about your sport. This is what makes your sport meaningful to you. When you have internal motivation you participate because you enjoy the activity; you play for the sake of playing. You participate because you like the process of learning about your sport and improving your skills. You enjoy the way it feels to overcome challenges. You even learn to embrace the things you don't like about your sport because it's all part of the journey. When your inner drive is strong, you can still become frustrated by mistakes or an off-day, but those disappointments fuel you to work on your game instead of taking away from your belief in yourself.

External motivation is when you are influenced to participate by things that are outside of you. When you are externally motivated you are driven to compete because of the positive feedback you receive or the negative consequences you want to avoid. You might participate for external rewards like getting compliments and recognition, winning championships and trophies, making friends and hanging out with like-minded people, receiving scholarships and paychecks, etc. You might also participate to avoid a negative consequence; getting cut from the team if you don't show up to practice, doing your rehabilitation exercises so you don't re-injure yourself, sticking to your training plan so you can finish your race, etc. All of these examples are external motivators; incentives that make it enticing to compete. External motivators are all of the other reasons you want to play, race, or compete other than just the pure joy of participating.

For Dick Hoyt, his main source of motivation is external. Dick and Rick Hoyt have been racing together since 1977. Because of circumstances during his birth, Rick was diagnosed with cerebral palsy, which affects his speech and his limb function. Rick is confined to a wheelchair and uses a special computer in order to communicate with the world around him. After you hear the story of Team Hoyt, you may decide that "confined" isn't the right word to use in reference to Rick Hoyt. Team Hoyt's racing adventure started when Rick told his Dad that he wanted to compete in a five-mile run. The run was a benefit for a classmate in Rick's school who had been paralyzed. Dick had never run more than a mile in his life, but they entered the benefit run and Dick ran five miles while pushing his son in a wheelchair. "Team Hoyt" was immediately formed when Rick told his Dad that while they were running he didn't feel like he was disabled anymore. Since that time, they have traveled across the country and competed in hundreds of races and not just running. Team Hoyt added triathlons to their race calendar including six Ironman distance triathlons. Dick Hoyt has no desire to race alone. His motivation is his son and he says, "He's the one who has motivated me, because if it wasn't for him, I wouldn't be out there competing."

Choosing a class because it is something you want to learn about and study is *internal motivation*. In contrast, taking a class because it is required to graduate is an example of *external motivation*. Showing up to practice because you love to play your sport and would take any opportunity to play is *internal motivation*. Showing up to practice because you don't want to lose or come in last is *external motivation*. If you're like me (and every athlete I've ever worked with) you're probably thinking — "Well I have some of both". The relationship between your internal and external motivation can be tricky. There are times when those external motivators can be beneficial to your internal motivation and times when those same external motivators can end up negatively affecting your internal motivation. External motivators aren't "bad"; it's when they compromise your internal motivation that you run into trouble. External motivators can be a great compliment to your internal motivation. For the athlete that loves participating in her sport, but doesn't love going to weight training, external motivation can be a great tool for getting through weight training. You might not be internally motivated to lift, but you are externally motivated to do it because you know that it will positively impact your ability to do what you love — what you are internally motivated to do.

Talking about the sources of motivation can sometimes lead people to ask, "Is it OK to want to win?" Of course it is! External motivation is an inherent part of sport. External motivation only starts to cause trouble when:

> A. You are *only* externally motivated.
> B. You perceive your external motivators to be *controlling*.

If you only compete because of the recognition you get, what happens when that recognition isn't forthcoming? It's like the quarterback/guitar player syndrome. In music and in sport there are certain roles that tend to get more spotlight than others. If you are the offensive lineman or the bass player, you might not get as much praise from the fans and the media. If the *only* reason you play football or play music is for that glory and you're not getting it, guess what happens to your motivation? But if you play offensive line or bass because you are passionate about it and you take pride in improving your skills, then guess what happens to your motivation when you aren't getting any love? Not getting recognition might be annoying, but it doesn't make you resent your teammates or band mates and make you want to quit. Here are some examples of how external motivators can be perceived as controlling:

- You've been working on improving a specific skill and you just saw the fruits of your labor pay off in competition. After the game, your coach (parent, spouse, teammate, etc.) says, "Hey that's great, but you should really work on…" and suddenly the wind is knocked from your sails. You *wanted* to improve because of your love for your sport and now you feel like you *have* to improve in order to get someone off your back or to get that positive reinforcement and recognition once again. Recognition has become a controlling factor instead of a complimentary one.

- You're an athlete moving up through the ranks and are finally getting paid to play your sport. You no longer have to worry about how to supplement your income and you can just focus on your training and competition. Things are great for a while, but then you start to feel some pressure to perform. Now you feel like you *have* to do well to earn the paycheck and pay your bills, to make your sponsors happy, and because everyone expects you to because you're getting paid. What once was a sign that you had made it, and accomplished your professional athletic goal, is now beginning to feel like a burden. Money is now a controlling factor instead of a complimentary one.

If you have passion for what you do, but feel that there are other motivational influences controlling you, it can be detrimental to your overall motivation. Feeling controlled by external motivators can make you feel angry and resentful, sucking all of the motivation right out of you. However, those same external motivators of recognition and money can also be complimentary to your motivation. If you have a strong internal drive and belief in your ability, then the same scenarios above may not be perceived as controlling. You might hear your coach give you feedback after a game on what to improve and instead of feeling crushed, you think, "Wow, my coach is really invested in my performance and thinks I'm ready to move it to the next level." You might experience people changing their expectations of you when you get a paycheck to play and instead of feeling pressure you think, "This paycheck is my proof that I am on the right path and it provides me with the opportunity to perform to my potential by taking away the stress of having to work on figuring out sponsors every year."

If you want to know whether or not you have any internal motivation, ask yourself; am I having fun? Do you enjoy any of the time that you are training and competing in your sport? That being said, training to be an athlete, to perform to your athletic potential, is not always going to be "fun". Being able to perform at a high level takes hard, disciplined, and dedicated work. If you think about your sport and are filled with angst, frustration, and dread… it's time to find your inner drive. The first exercise in this chapter helps you to explore both your internal and external motivators for participating in your sport to make sure that your external motivators are complimenting your motivation rather than diminishing it.

Do I Feel Capable, In Control, and Connected?

By now you are probably realizing that motivation is more than just the direction and intensity of your effort. You know that there are two sources of motivation, internal and external, and you also know that external motivators can either enhance or diminish your internal motivation. Now we are going to move onto the factors that can influence your inner drive. There are three main *factors* that can either facilitate or wreak havoc with your motivation:

- Feeling you are skilled or unskilled at your sport.
- Feeling in control or out of control of your decision to compete.
- Feeling you belong or don't belong to the group.

Do I Feel Capable?

Your feelings about your capability in your sport will influence your level of motivation. Ask yourself: *Do I feel like this is something I can be good at?* If you believe that by putting in the time and effort that this is something you can excel at, that belief can positively affect your motivation. Going back to the earlier motivational scenarios of staying in crosswalks, doing well in college, and preparing for competition demonstrates how your beliefs influence your actions. In all of these scenarios, the actions stem from the motivation to move toward something or move away from something. If you believe it will hurt if a car hits you, then that belief will influence your motivation, and that motivation will influence the decisions you make and the actions you take. In this scenario, you are motivated to not get hit by a car, so you go to the crosswalk and wait until you know it is safe to cross. If you believe that maybe it wouldn't hurt that bad or that you could outrun a car, you probably wouldn't be motivated to walk the extra block to get to the crosswalk. You believe that getting into the college of your choice will help you to accomplish your career goals so you are motivated to do what it takes to get into that college. If you believe that whether or not you get into college has no bearing on whether or not you get your dream job, then you may not be as motivated to go to class, do your homework, and study for your exams. If you believe that the training plan you have set out will help you to accomplish your goals, then you will be motivated to stick to that training plan. If you believe that you can do well in competition regardless of the training you put in, then you might be more likely to skip a few practices. Your motivation is tied to your beliefs, therefore your beliefs influence which direction you choose to go.

In the simplest terms, if you think you can be good at something, you'll be more motivated to do it; if you think that you won't be good at something, you'll be less motivated to do it. You're directed by your beliefs. Oftentimes when people assume that someone has a lack of motivation, what they actually lack is confidence. We all want to be good at something. If you try out a new skill and see yourself improve, your brain gets the message, "Hey check it out, I worked on this and I got better." Seeing yourself improve means you will be more motivated to keep working. You believe that your hard work will pay off with improvements in your performance; therefore you are motivated to continue to work at it. However, if you try out a new skill and struggle to improve, your brain gets the message "Hey man, it doesn't matter what I do — I am destined to suck at this," then you will be much less likely to continue working. Here is an example of the frustration experienced by a college freshman during pre-season:

> *I'm doing everything that coach is telling me to do. I'm working so hard to improve my mechanics. I even come in early and put in the extra work, but no matter how much I do I'm not improving. I feel like I'm never going to win a starting position. Why should I even bother if it's not going to work?*

When struggling to improve on a skill, you feel like no matter how hard you work, you are not improving, so why even bother. You look around and see other people improving and it makes you feel even worse. When you don't feel capable, it can impact how much effort you put out, as well as impact your desire to want to show up at all.

Do I Feel In Control?

An additional factor that can impact your level of motivation is whether or not you feel like you are in control of your choice. Ask yourself: *Do I feel like I am in control of my decision to be here?* When I lost my motivation to rock climb, I felt like I had no control over my choice to climb. Even though it was all in my head, I felt like every time my husband suggested a climbing trip that I was being forced to climb against my will. When you perceive that competing in your sport is not by your choice, it will affect your motivation. You need to know that you are free to do as you choose and that *you are making the choice to compete.* Take away control and you compromise your internal motivation. Here are some examples of situations that can affect your perception of control:

- Your coach is constantly switching around your position. You feel like you have no idea when you'll be in the game or what position you'll be playing.
- You've hired a coach and you feel like you're being forced to follow a cookie-cutter training plan and you're not sure that the plan will work to help you accomplish your goals.
- You feel like you're a slave to your anxiety and there is nothing you can do to make things better. You love your sport and even though you are miserable, you force yourself to compete.
- You feel like everyone else in your life has a vested interest in you continuing to compete and you can't untangle yourself to figure out if this is something you really want to do.

As you know from the last chapter, nothing stresses you out more than feeling like you are powerless. It's important to assess whether or not you really have no control, or whether it is just your perception of having no control. Even when there are situations that you have no control of, you can still govern how you react to them and how they ultimately affect you. When I lost my motivation to rock climb, I felt like someone else was pulling the strings. I had control, but my *perception* was that I had no control. You need to put the power back into your own hands.

Do I Feel Connected?

The final factor is a social one. Ask yourself: *Do I feel like I am a part of this group?* Whether you are on a team or participate in an individual sport, do you feel like you are a part of that culture? On a very basic level, as humans we have an innate desire to be connected to others. We want to have a valued place in the world; to feel that we belong. Like anything, there are different factors that influence whether or not we feel connected:

- Do you get sincere positive and evaluative feedback from your coach?
- Do you feel like you have friends on your team?
- Are you surrounded by other people who are motivated to train and participate in your sport?
- Do you have a support system that empowers you to accomplish your goals?

All of these can help facilitate your own internal motivation. When you don't feel connected you won't be as motivated to be a part of your team or your sport.

All three of these factors can have an impact on your level of internal motivation. It's not as simple as a light switch where if you have all three factors the light is on and if you don't have them the light is off, but if you can say:

Yes, I feel capable. Yes, I feel in control. Yes, I feel connected.

it will positively impact your internal motivation. When your internal motivation is strong, your external motivators will be more likely to compliment your motivation. When your internal motivation is high, you are less likely to get derailed by the inevitable challenges and setbacks you will face as an athlete. When your internal motivation is high, you will be better set up to receive feedback and make improvements on your performance. If you feel you *aren't* capable, you *aren't* in control, and you *aren't* connected ... you won't be sticking around for long.

What Does it Mean When Your Motivation is Low?

Since motivation is so complex, having low motivation can be an indicator of several different things. Sometimes you can feel low on motivation and don't know what to attribute it to. Here are some examples that can lead to a dip in your motivation:

You're frustrated with your performance

Your motivation is low because you're experiencing a slump in your performance. If you are dealing with any kind of performance anxiety, you are also possibly performing better in training than in competition. You see it in training, so you know that you are capable, but you're not performing when it counts. When you aren't performing to your potential and feel like you have tried to make improvements to no avail, it can affect your motivation. When you are in this position you might begin to try too hard and try to force things, or start to lose hope that anything will change and become so frustrated that you stop trying altogether. In this situation your low motivation is a sign that you are frustrated with your performance.

You need a break

Your motivation is low because you need a vacation from your sport. Length of season and monotonous training can lead to low motivation as well. If you are feeling a dip in your motivation, it might be a sign that you need to take a break. When you think about life in general — why do people need to take a break from something? It's usually because they are bored, overworked, or just need to re-charge their batteries. As in life, so goes in sport. You need breaks. This might mean actually taking time off, or it may mean changing things up. If your motivation is low because you're bored, then you might need a change of scenery for your next training day or you might need to add in some cross-training to change things up. If you are feeling overworked or feel like you need to re-charge the batteries, your low motivation is a sign that you need to take some time off.

You need support

We are affected by the support, or lack of support we have surrounding us. When you are having issues with coaches, teammates, and even family and friends, it can negatively affect your motivation. Having people that support you and believe in you is essential for performing to your potential. You need different types of support, and making sure you have *all* of the assistance you need is key to building up a strong support system. (You'll get a chance to work on building your support system in Chapter Ten.)

Finding Your Inner Drive

Some athletes contact me because they are thinking about quitting their sport; they aren't seeing the results they are used to seeing, they aren't having fun anymore, and it's affecting their motivation to train and compete. When you have been dealing with performance anxiety for a while, it can begin to take a toll on your motivation. I've had athletes and parents of athletes that start to question whether or not it is even healthy for them to continue in their sport when it is causing so much angst. You can start to question whether or not it is even worth it to compete, but you keep going back because there is a part of you that still loves your sport. More often than not, when you learn to manage your anxiety and your performance starts to turn around, your motivation starts to turn around as well. I've worked with countless athletes on the verge of quitting that end up regaining their motivation and passion for their sport. Many even come back and have the best season of their lives because they now have the tools they need to manage their anxiety. But is it the chicken or the egg? Do you need to improve your performance in order to be motivated or do you need to be motivated in order to improve your performance? The answer is — both. Working on the exercises at the end of this chapter will help you re-connect with your inner drive (a.k.a., working on your motivation to improve your performance). Working on the exercises in the subsequent chapters will help you manage your anxiety (a.k.a., improve performance and enhance motivation).

If you completed the Peak Performance Vision tool from the last chapter you will have a glimpse into your inner drive. Having that internal motivation is a powerful foundation to work from, but because it's natural for your motivation to ebb and flow, you need some other tools to fill in the gaps. There are different types of tools to help with different types of motivational issues. I find that there are three different categories that these tools fall into: motivation, inspiration, and commitment. Motivation starts you on your path, inspiration keeps you going, and commitment gets you to the end. Tools for motivation help you discover why you do it — what drives you to participate in your sport? These tools can help you assess your level of motivation and your sources of motivation. However, sometimes we don't need to assess our global motivation; sometimes what we need is some rejuvenation, a little fire in the belly (or a little kick in the butt!). In those circumstances what you need are tools for inspiration, like the high school swimmer that has to get up and train in the early morning hours before school, or the triathlete with a full-time job that has to find time to train for their Ironman race. These tools — motivation, inspiration, and commitment — can help us reconnect with our own inner drive. They help rekindle the passion you already have for your sport. Other times you need tools that help with determination and discipline — ways to help with commitment to your sport and your goals. These are tools that will be covered in the next chapter. The tools in this chapter will help you access your inner drive and give you the inspiration you need to both increase your motivation and get it moving in the right direction.

Chapter 2: Take-Aways

- Motivation affects every aspect of training and performance. When you work on your motivation, you are working on the foundation of your performance.
- Having a strong inner drive will help you to meet challenges head on, keep you on track towards your goals, and enhance your enjoyment of your sport.

- External motivators can be complimentary as long as you have a strong internal motivation and you don't perceive the external motivators to be in control.

- It's normal for your motivation to fluctuate and change over time, but a dip in motivation is also a sign you should pay attention to. Being able to diagnose why your motivation is low will help you choose the right tools to address it.

- When you feel capable, in control, and connected, it will positively influence your motivation. Having these factors helps increase both your effort and your enjoyment of your sport.

Chapter 2: Tools

Tool: What's My Motivation?

This exercise is a motivational survey. You will answer a series of questions related to your motivation in order to get a solid grasp of why you participate in your sport and what impacts your motivation. Give yourself some dedicated time to really address the questions. It may be tempting, but don't skip questions. You can answer them in any order that you want, but be sure to answer them all. If you need to you can go back and look up internal and external motivators from earlier in the chapter to refresh your memory and get the ideas flowing. Remember there are worksheets that you can access at www.carriecheadle.com to write out your answers, otherwise you can just write your answers in a notebook and add them to your mental skills binder.

1. Internal motivation: Why do you compete? What do you love about your sport?
2. External motivation: What are your external motivators? What other benefits do you get from participating?
3. How do you know when your motivation is low?
4. How do your external motivators compliment your internal motivation?
5. How do your external motivators take away from your internal motivation?
6. What are some ways that you can increase your feelings of confidence and control?
7. What are some mental and physical skills you would like to improve on?
8. What is one step you can take that you haven't already taken in order to move towards improving those skills?

Tool: Inspired Athlete

For this exercise you will be creating your go-to list of inspiration. There are four different tasks you will need to do in order to complete your *Inspired Athlete* tool. It will take some time, but once it is complete you will have an amazing tool to draw motivation from when you need it most.

Step 1: *Top Five Inspirational Quotes* ... Inspirational quotes can serve as your mantras throughout the season. Quotes that truly speak to you can evoke powerful feelings just by reading them. A few of my favorites to get you started:

"The harder you work, the harder it is to surrender." —Vince Lombardi

"Adversity causes some men to break; others to break records."
—William A. Ward

"I am building a fire, and every day I train, I add more fuel. At just the right moment, I light the match." —Mia Hamm

Inspirational quotes can be fantastic reminders of our values and beliefs all wrapped up into one or two perfect sentences. Come up with your list of top five quotes and post them up where you can see them or memorize them so you can call on them during those moments when you need them the most.

Step 2: *Top Five Inspirational Movies* ... Movies can be a great source of inspiration. Movies like *Miracle* and *Breaking Away* share great stories that have the power to move you and inspire you to action. Create your own movie library with your top five all-time inspirational sports films. When your motivation is low, take a break with a movie night.

Step 3: *Top Five Inspirational Songs* ... Music has the ability to impact our emotional state and physiological intensity. Your entire mood and energy can change when a particular song comes on. Make a list of the five songs that pump you up the most. Whether it's hard rock or techno, select songs that get you excited as soon as you hear the first note.

Step 4: *Top Five Personal Highlights* ... Create a list of your top sport achievements. Write out a list of five (or add more if you want!) accomplishments that you feel good about. (For me, those might include the time I made a 90-foot putt in disc golf or the first time I was able to confidently ride up Chair 10 – the one with the skull-and-crossbones sign at Kirkwood Mountain Resort!) They don't all have to be about outcome. Your best performances can be on the list, but you can also have other achievements like overcoming setbacks and performance improvements.

Step 5: After you complete each task you will compile the lists into one fabulous *Inspired Athlete* document. Don't just make the list, use it as a resource. Pull it out when you start to feel a dip in your motivation and pick something off of the list to focus on. Read through your accomplishments, listen to a song, watch a movie — recalibrate your motivation. Of course, this list will change over time. After you have created your initial list, the off-season is a great time to make any changes or additions.

chapter 3

CHOOSING YOUR DESTINATION

"If you don't know where you're going, you might end up some place else."
—Yogi Berra, Hall of Fame baseball player

When you think about athletes accomplishing goals you usually envision the big moments. You imagine the Olympian standing on the podium, lowering her head so the gold medal can be placed around her neck. You see tears in her eyes and know she just accomplished a life-long goal. Or maybe you envision the last pitch of the final inning during a championship game and see the cheers of an elated winning team as they rush the field. You see the triumph in their eyes and know they will remember that moment forever. You see these athletes accomplish their goals, but don't always see the path it took for them to get there. As a fan or spectator we don't always see the thousands of steps that occurred between the moment they started participating in their sport to the moment they got the gold or won the championship game. Setting and working towards goals can be a powerful motivational tool. Deliberately setting goals helps drive your energy and effort in one direction. Monitoring your progress on goals can enhance your confidence as you experience successes along your path.

Now that you have the "why" from the previous chapter it's time to figure out the "what". What do you want to accomplish? In other words, where do you want to go and how will you get there? Is it completing your first Olympic-distance triathlon? Or winning a starting position? Bringing home the National Championship title? Despite the positive benefits of goal-setting, some athletes still avoid setting formal goals. Those athletes feel that when they set goals they increase the pressure they put on themselves to perform. Athletes will tell me, "I don't like to set goals for my performance, it just makes me feel more nervous. All I can think about is what happens if I don't accomplish my goal." Other athletes have experienced being told what their goals are. They had no input into the process and therefore had no personal connection to the goal. Some athletes just feel like it isn't necessary to set goals in order to play their sport and believe the time and energy spent on goal setting isn't worth it.

The truth is that goal setting is an essential tool for any athlete looking to improve their performance. Goals will remain unfulfilled dreams unless action is taken. Goals can help direct energy and focus. Goal setting is not wishing and hoping; it is doing. You only have to watch the movie "Rudy" to know the power of having a goal. The movie (which I highly recommend you add to your inspirational movie list!) tells the true story of Daniel "Rudy" Ruettiger. Rudy grew up watching Notre Dame Football like it was a religion. Each time the game came on, he wasn't just watching a football game; he was dreaming of the day he would be a student at Notre Dame. His story is a beautiful and honest depiction of what it's like to take a dream and make it a goal. His goal was to get accepted into Notre Dame to study and play football for the Fighting Irish. It seemed like a pretty lofty goal considering his academic background and the fact that he was 5'6" and 165 pounds, but Rudy kept putting one foot in front of the other. Despite constantly receiving messages from the people in his life that he would never accomplish his goal, Rudy had a clear vision of what he wanted to do and carved out a path in order to do it. Rudy encountered many setbacks along the way, but he chose his destination and wouldn't stop until he got there. Daniel Ruettiger, the *real* Rudy even proclaims, "Never quit. Don't ever quit … If you quit you'll regret it forever." The reason he was successful was because he knew exactly what he wanted, exactly why he wanted it, and knew exactly what he needed to be successful.

———

The reality is that you are always setting goals. You may not think of it in such formal terms, but you're constantly working towards things you've set out to accomplish. Whether it's showing up for practice on time or working towards a new personal record, energy is being put into goal setting every day and some days that energy is being utilized more effectively than others. The reason this topic is so important is because *you gauge your success based on the goals you set for yourself* so it is imperative that you put thought into what those goals are and how you will go about setting and striving for them. In order for goals to be successful and actually improve performance, you need to be setting the right types of goals that cover both the direction you want to go and the steps you need to take in order to achieve success.

Types of Goals

An effective goal-setting program is just like planning a road trip. You've packed your bags, there's gas in the car; you're ready to go. Now you're sitting in the driver's seat, you start the engine and slowly realize you have no idea where you're headed. The first thing you need to do when you're headed out on a road trip is to figure out where you want to go. If you don't know where you're going, then you certainly won't know how to get there. Just like a road trip, your goal plan needs to include all of the necessary steps to take you from point A to point B. When creating your goal plan, there are three types of goals you need to set: long-term goals, short-term goals, and process goals. The most effective goal-setting programs will address all three types of goals.

- Long-term goals help guide your short-term goals in the direction you want to go. An example of this might be to compete in your first triathlon in four months time.
- Short-term goals help you stay on track with accomplishing your long-term goals. Following up from the long-term goal, an example of a short-term goal would be to join a triathlon club that offers swim clinics and choose a training plan.
- Process goals help keep you focused on the actions needed to attain your short-term goals. In this case, examples of process goals would be to block off time in your schedule to accommodate your training plan and work on breathing and pacing during swim practice to improve endurance and confidence.

This is what goal setting is all about, developing the vision and defining the steps it will take to accomplish the goal.

Long-term Goals

The first step in creating your goal plan is to figure out where you are headed. In other words, when you look down the road of your athletic life — where do you see yourself going? What do you want your sport career to look like? Without knowing what you are working towards, you can get stuck just going through the motions without having a real purpose. Having that destination in mind can help guide your everyday behavior and make sure it's in line with what you really want to accomplish. When you have that long-term goal, you know what you are working for, which can have a powerful impact on your motivation to both create and stick to your short-term and process goals.

As an athlete, your long-term goal might entail getting rookie of the year, getting a starting position on your team, upgrading to the next level in your sport, getting a personal record, winning a specific competition, or even entering your first race. It might also entail how you want to feel when you show up to a big event or how you want to feel at the end of the season. Knowing your final destination can be a powerful motivator and ensure that you keep driving down the road in the direction you need to go. Having a solid and specific long-term goal can also help when you encounter challenges along the way. When you are on a road trip, you could get a flat tire, run out of gas, or hit a dead end, but when you know exactly where you are headed, roadblocks don't end the trip — they are just a temporary delay because your final destination always remains within your mind's eye.

Short-term Goals

On a road trip, you can't just head out the door and hop in the car; you need a road map to help plan your route and show you how to get where you're going. To accomplish this task you need to define your short-term goals. Short-term goals provide specific and measurable steps that must be completed in order to accomplish your long-term goal. If you are headed out on a road trip that leaves from California and your final destination is New

York, you can't get there without driving through many other states first. If your long-term goal includes winning a starting position on your team, your short-term goals will define the milestones you need to accomplish to get there. Do you know exactly what your coach wants to see from you to get the starting position? What skills do you need to improve on? If you're your long-term goal includes upgrading to the next level in your sport, what needs to happen first? What are you not doing now that you need to be doing in order to make a move in that direction? Effective short-term goals are objectives that should answer the question "What do I need to do in order to achieve my long-term goal?" Your long-term goal tells you where to go and your short-term goals tell you how to get there. They provide you with the steps it will take to make it to your final destination.

Process Goals

Once you have your destination and your map, what else is left? You still need to figure out how you will be spending your time each day; you need to define your process goals. What do you need to do in order to accomplish your short-term goals? Your process goals are the strategies and specific actions you will take to realize your short-term goals. How many hours will you drive each day? How much money do you want to spend on each meal? Where are you going to get gas? Process goals focus on execution and behaviors related to your performance. They keep you engaged on the task at hand and keep you focused on what is in your control. If your long-term goal is to win a starting position on your team and you've defined the skills your coach wants you to improve on, what steps do you need to take to improve on those skills? If your long-term goal is to move up to the next level in your sport and you know what milestones need to be hit along the way, what steps do you need to take to reach each milestone? Your process goals help define how you need to be spending your time if you want to reach your destination. If you achieve your process goals, you are more likely to get the outcome that you want.

———

Many people hold back on creating a clear vision of what they want out of fear they might not get it. This is the fear that whispers, "What if I put everything on the line, tell everyone in my life what I really want, and fall flat on my face? What if I say what I really want and I can't do it?" For some people, having a clear vision makes them feel anxious because it makes them feel vulnerable. It makes them feel like they have just turned themselves inside out and now everyone can see what's really on the inside — blood, guts, and all. Creating a clear vision, or choosing your destination, takes courage and passion. It takes big thinking and forces you to shift from "What if I can't?" to "Why not!?" Some athletes have no problem developing their vision. To them, that's the fun part. For them, the bigger challenge is figuring out how to get there; getting down to 'brass tacks' and defining the actual steps it will take. The high school athlete that says, "I definitely want to play in college," but doesn't understand the steps it will take to make that goal a reality. Athletes that hold back, because of that fear, never find out what they are truly capable of. They will always wonder, in the back of their minds, about what might have been.

All three types of goals play an important role in creating a path to the desired destination. Zoom out and you can get a picture of the whole map. You can get a sense of where things are and where you are in relation to them. Zoom in a little and you can see where the next immediate destination is on the road trip. You can see what towns you will drive through and how long it will take to get there. Zoom in some more and you will see the exact streets you need to take and where you will fuel up along the way. Each type of goal supports the other and is necessary for an effective goal setting plan.

The Secret Goal

The reason it is important to spend time on learning the skill of setting goals and having an effective goal setting strategy is because you gauge your success based on the goals you set. More to the point, you gauge your success based on whether you feel like you accomplished or failed at meeting your goal. If you have only developed a vision, but haven't spent time on developing your objectives and strategies, you have not set yourself up with an effective goal plan. However, *in your mind you have set a goal and may feel like you have failed to accomplish that goal, which affects your level of motivation and confidence.* What you have actually done is failed to set an effective goal. The other problem I see athletes run into is when they have a "secret goal". We all have secret goals from time to time; the goal that we *really* want to accomplish, but won't admit to. I talk to athletes a lot about their "secret goals" or as one of my athletes puts it, her "hidden agenda". For example, let's say a triathlete that has been racing successfully at Olympic Distance triathlons has decided to enter her first long course triathlon. She has set a challenging yet realistic goal for herself to finish within a certain time, but her "secret goal" is to finish in the top third of her age group. The reason this idea of the secret goal is so important is because *the secret goal is the goal you gauge your success on.* She might accomplish her stated goal and even surpass it, but feel disappointed because she is gauging her success based on the fact that she didn't accomplish her secret goal.

There are many reasons why an athlete might have a secret goal. You have your stated goal, the goal you share with people out loud, but you actually have another goal you are holding onto in the back of your mind. It may be that the secret goal is what you really want to shoot for, but isn't quite realistic (like the above example). However, you're secretly hoping that is the goal you will achieve. It could also be that you want the secret goal to be the true goal, but are afraid to say it. You aren't confident in your ability to accomplish it or are afraid of being embarrassed or disappointed if you don't. Athletes may put additional pressure on themselves once they admit their true goal out loud so they keep it to themselves and downplay what their goals truly are.

You need to be honest with yourself about what your real goal is. When you discover that you have a secret goal there are only two things you can do: you can accept that your stated goal is what you really want to achieve, or accept that your secret goal is what you really want to achieve. Often, your secret goal is what you want to achieve, but there is a discrepancy between your secret goal and what you are actually capable of achieving at this point in time. This can be especially challenging when you can see that at some point it will be realistic for you. I was working with an athlete that knew a spot on the podium was just within his grasp. He was on his way to making that goal a reality, but also knew that he needed to fine-tune his training to be able to make that final push. Every time he raced, that podium spot was his secret goal and each time he raced and didn't get that podium spot it felt like a punch in the stomach. If you continue to gauge your success based on that goal and you don't accomplish it, it will negatively impact your confidence even if you accomplished 100% of what was possible for you on that day.

When you discover you have a secret goal, you have to either commit or accept. You need to *commit* to doing what it takes to accomplish the goal you really want or *accept* that your stated goal is your true goal because that is what is realistic for you right now. Even knowing all of this, I will still succumb to having secret goals. When I got back into trail running after a two-year hiatus, I signed up for my first race, excited just to get back into it. My goal was to just sign up and complete the race. Apparently I had a secret goal because by the end of the race I was disappointed in my performance and then when I saw my result, I was *pissed*. I had a secret goal and didn't even know it. But I also did not commit to the kind of training necessary to accomplish that secret goal so I used that information moving forward and tweaked my training plan to be more competitive for the next race. If you realize you had a secret goal after an event, you need to make sure you are gauging your success on your stated goal and be proud of your accomplishment. Then you can analyze your feelings about your event to decide what you really want to achieve for the next event and assess whether you are ready to commit to that goal or if you need to stick to your stated goal.

Why People Fail to Set Effective Goals

When I was a kid, my absolute favorite video game on Atari 2600 was *Pitfall*. (For those of you born after the year 1985, Atari 2600 is one of the dinosaurs of the home videogame console.) In the game you had to move Pitfall Harry through different obstacles in the jungle while collecting treasure along the way before your time ran out. I loved maneuvering that little guy; swinging on the vines and navigating my way through the dangers of the jungle. The pitfalls were many; you had to avoid alligators, scorpions, and the dreaded quicksand. It was thrilling to encounter the dangers and I felt triumphant as I conquered them. In the game, I learned where the challenges were and figured out exactly how to avoid them. I knew they were coming so I was prepared and knew what I needed to do. I didn't even care about the treasures along the way — I just wanted to conquer the challenges of the jungle.

When you are on a path moving towards a goal, it's just like playing the game of Pitfall. It's not enough to just know what types of goals to set. There are many other factors involved with setting an effective goal plan, a plan that actually sees you accomplishing your goal. You may not encounter alligators and scorpions, like I did while playing the video game, but there are five main pitfalls I see athletes fall into that can be easily avoided if you learn what they are and know exactly what to do to avoid them.

Pitfall #1: Setting Too Many Goals

In order to truly improve performance and effect lasting change, you can't go after everything all at once. You have to choose one or two goals that you are completely committed to and focus on those. We don't have the energy or resources available to give everything we have to ten or twenty different goals. Set yourself up to be successful with your goal setting by choosing which goals you *really* want to focus on *right now*. Your life is a reflection of the choices you make and you are in control of making those choices. Decide what is important and spend your energy on that.

Pitfall #2: Setting Goals That Are Too General

The more specific you are with the path you need to take to accomplish your goals, the more likely you will be to take the necessary steps to make it happen. When you set goals that are too general, it's like saying "Wouldn't it be nice if I could improve my performance?" Stop *daydreaming* and start *doing*. If you set goals that are too general you are setting yourself up to not accomplish your goals. It's one thing to say, "I want to be a better swimmer" and another thing entirely to say, "I want to improve my 1.5k swim time by three minutes. To accomplish this I will start swimming more consistently by joining the masters swim class that meets on Tuesdays and Thursdays. To work further on my skills, I will I will research swim clinics this week and register for one by next Friday." Move yourself from wishing to doing by being specific.

Pitfall #3: Setting Goals That Are Too Easy or Too Hard

It seems like it should go without saying that you need to set goals that are realistic, goals that are within your ability to achieve. If athletes set goals that aren't realistic for them to achieve, they may get frustrated and abandon the goal altogether instead of coming up with a more realistic goal. What's fascinating is that research has shown that athletes will also abandon their goal if it is too easy. Think about a goal that would be amazing to achieve, but is most definitely out of your reach. Then think about a goal that is a no-brainer, absolutely 100% within your reach. Now pick something in between. Your level of effort will be highest if you choose a goal that is challenging, but realistic. Choose a goal that you would have to work hard to accomplish and would feel like a real victory if you did.

Pitfall #4: Not Preparing for Obstacles

Another major pitfall of goal setting is not effectively dealing with obstacles you will encounter along the way. You hit a brick wall and instead of finding a way around it you sit down and end your journey right there. Heather Dorniden was running for the University of Minnesota at the 2008 Big 10 Indoor Track Championships when she hit her wall. She was running the 600m and was running a beautiful race when with one lap to go she started to move to the inside of the track, cut in too close to another runner, then tripped and fell. You could hear the immediate gasp of the entire crowd as she fell to the ground. Without hesitating, Dorniden got up and continued running. On that final lap she quickly gained on the competition to the deafening cheers of the crowd and in the final stretch she overcame the other runners to win the race. A different athlete may have thought that her race was over and abandoned the goal. For Dorniden, it was just an obstacle to overcome.

Setbacks are inevitable. They are a part of the journey. Goals need to be flexible and adjustable if you are to continue moving forward on your path. As I tell my athletes, one of the most important skills you can have when it comes to goal setting is the ability to adjust. Your goals aren't carved in stone. Goal setting is a fluid and moving process. The ability to adjust, tweak, and refine goals is a part of being successful with those goals. There may be times when it becomes necessary to adjust your goal due to circumstances that are out of your control. Your ability to make that adjustment means the difference between persevering and giving up on your goals.

Pitfall #5: Neglecting to Get Feedback

One of the most neglected aspects of goal setting is reflecting on the process and getting feedback. You put in the effort and energy to create the goals at the outset of the journey and then never look at them or touch them again. In order for you to see the progress you are making towards your goals, you need to receive feedback along the way. If you don't have a clear idea of how you are progressing, you won't be able to make the necessary adjustments to make sure you are staying on track. Reflecting on your progress allows you to develop knowledge-in-action. You gain the knowledge and build on that knowledge to impact your progress towards your goals and your performance. (We'll get into more specifics on reflection and feedback in Chapter Eight.) Creating accountability by setting specific times to check in on your goal progress can enhance your confidence and motivation and keep you on your goal path.

Are You Committed to Your Goals?

Now that you know the way to create a successful goal plan, how to tackle your secret goals, and what pitfalls to avoid on your journey, it's time to address the foundation beneath it all. Having specific goals can propel you to action, *but only if you are committed to those goals*. Is this something you really want? Are you willing to do what it takes to get there? In the last chapter you learned that your level of motivation will impact how much energy and effort you are willing to put into your sport. The same is true for the goals you set for yourself. The impact your goals have on your performance depends on your level of commitment to your goals. Here are some factors that can contribute to your level of commitment:

Who set the goal?

When someone else sets a goal for you versus you setting a goal for yourself, it can influence how committed you are to accomplishing that goal. When you perceive you aren't in control of your goals and feel they aren't realistic for you, you won't be motivated to try to accomplish them. If you are in a situation where goals will be assigned to you, you need to cover a couple bases in order to have the same level of commitment you would if you had set them yourself. You need to find your own connection to that goal and take ownership over your own desire to achieve it. If you understand the purpose of the goal, you will be more committed to working on it. When you play a team sport you need to be committed both to your team goals and your individual goals and understand how they can positively impact each other. If someone is assigning you a goal and you aren't a participant in that process, make yourself a part of it by taking the time to ask yourself:

- What is the purpose of this goal?
- Why is this goal important to me?
- What would it mean to me to accomplish this goal?
- How will working towards this goal help my performance?

Don't think about how other people would answer the question – taking ownership of the goal means answering and understanding these questions for yourself.

Are you confident?

Your level of confidence in your ability to accomplish your goal will affect your level of commitment towards that goal. If your level of confidence is low, you will be less committed to working on your goal. If your level of confidence is high, if you believe that you have a good chance of succeeding with accomplishing your goal, your effort will be higher and you will persevere longer when you encounter challenges on your goal path. If you imagine yourself failing, you will be less committed to your goal and be more likely to quit when faced with obstacles and adversity. Once you have set a goal, ask yourself these questions to assess your level of confidence:

- How confident am I in my ability to accomplish my goal?
- What would help me feel more confident?
- What kind of support do I need in order to work on this?

Your answers to these questions will provide you with information on how to enhance your confidence and adjust your goal if needed.

Do you have accountability?

When you are on a team, there is some built in accountability to work on your goals in order to stay competitive and improve your performance. Having accountability can help you stay on track with your goals. It provides a reminder of what you really want to accomplish when you get bogged down with other things. Accountability can be a source of goal support. Knowing your coach holds you to a certain standard and that your actions also impact your teammates can be a factor in sticking to your goals. If you compete in an individual sport, you may have to find ways to create some accountability to support your commitment to your goal. Accountability can come in many forms. Writing down your goals and posting them up can be a form of accountability. Having a coach that you have to report your goal progress to is a form of accountability. Having a goal buddy, someone you will verbally share your goal and your progress with — someone that will check in with you to see if you are doing what you said you were going to do — can help keep you committed to your goal. Even creating reinforcers like some kind of incentive or reward — this could be getting yourself a new piece of equipment or planning a celebration dinner — for hitting your milestones is a form of accountability as well. Assess your accountability by asking yourself:

- What kind of accountability do I have?
- What can I do to increase my accountability?
- Who could I ask to be my goal buddy?

Accountability is an added measure that helps you stay responsible to your chosen goals. Create ways to keep yourself responsible to the goals that you want to complete.

Setting Effective Goals

Having an effective goal setting plan will help contribute to your feelings of competence and control. Having an ineffective goal setting plan will contribute to feelings of doubt and anxiety. There is a tendency is for people to get frustrated and possibly give up when there is a discrepancy between where they are now and where they want to be. Many times, the cause of that discrepancy has to do with an incomplete goal-setting plan. Take the triathlete that wants to compete in her first triathlon, but is terrified by the idea of an open water swim. Her desire to compete overpowers her fear and she decides to go for it, but during the race ends up panicking in the water and has to head back to the shore. She set herself up to fail because she failed to create a goal plan that would see her to the end of the race. When you understand the elements involved in setting effective goals you can create a goal path that feeds your confidence and motivation versus feeding your anxiety, doubt, and fear.

Just as people are motivated to move towards something or away from something, people set goals because they want to succeed at something or have a desire to avoid failing at something. If reading about committing to your goal is anxiety provoking, you are not alone. If you tend to put pressure on yourself to succeed and try to avoid failure at all costs, the idea of setting concrete goals may be pushing you right out of your comfort zone. For some people, just the act of setting goals seems to increase expectations and therefore increase the pressure to perform. They believe "Now that I've set a goal, I have to accomplish it." Not setting specific goals is a way for us to preserve our ego and suppress our feelings of anxiety. If you don't set a goal, then you don't have to risk the possibility of failing to accomplish that goal. It's easier on our egos to not set goals and just go along for the ride and see what happens. But like Mike Ditka once said, "How many successful people have you ever heard say, 'I just make it up as I go along?' I can't think of one." In order for you to work towards accomplishing your goal you have to be willing to face the possibility of not accomplishing it. It takes courage to put yourself out there and say what you really want. You wouldn't hold yourself back from going on an amazing road trip because you might get a flat tire, so don't hold yourself back from going after the goal you really want to accomplish because you might encounter setbacks and stumble along the way.

Every day you make a choice to take a step closer towards your goals, remain where you are, or move further away from them. When you are committed to your goals, you increase the probability that those goals will have a positive impact on your performance. Goals are markers along the journey of competing in your sport. The attainment of the goal isn't the only reward — it's also the continual process of moving towards them. Goals focus your energy and efforts in the direction you want to move. Setting goals — accomplishments that mark your progress — is a continual process. It's not just the goal, or the destination that's important, but choosing a destination and moving towards it. Without defined goals you may not move in that direction as quickly or you may not move in that direction at all. If you feel like goal setting hasn't worked for you in the past, chances are you haven't actually implemented an effective goal-setting program. *Yes,* it takes work and *yes,* it is worth it. Just ask gold medalist Dara Torres who at the age of 41, competed in her fifth Olympics and brought home three silver medals. She knew exactly what it would take in order to accomplish her goals and created the goal plan she needed to make it happen. The story of her incredible accomplishments during the 2008 Beijing Olympics is still a great source of inspiration. She showed the world that the only limits we have are the ones we put on ourselves. Effective goal-setting is a skill and the more you do it, the easier it gets to set and track your goals and see those hard earned improvements to your performance.

Chapter 3: Take-Aways

- Whether conscious or not, you are always setting goals and you gauge your success based on how you did relative to the goals you set. Make sure you are setting those goals deliberately and effectively.
- Be sure your goal plan includes all three types of goals. Set yourself up to be successful with your goals by knowing exactly where you are headed and exactly how you will get there.
- Avoid the pitfalls of goal-setting by choosing one or two goals to focus on that are both challenging and realistic, being specific with your goals, planning for potential obstacles, and getting feedback along the way.
- Your level of commitment dictates your level of effort. It's not enough to know *how* you will accomplish your goals, but *why* do you want to accomplish them?
- There will be setbacks along the way. The ability to adjust your goals is an essential skill to have in order to continue moving forward on your goal path.

Chapter 3: Tools

Tool: Goal Plan

You are about to embark on an exciting journey and the first step is to decide where you want to go. It's time to create the road map to your goals. To practice the skill of goal-setting, pick just one goal — one destination to focus on. You might want to travel to Boston *and* New York (and you will!), but for now, which destination comes first? Follow these steps to create a road map to your destination:

Step 1: To help develop your vision, grab a piece of paper and write out your answers to the following questions:
What is a goal that would be absolutely incredible to accomplish this year, but is too unrealistic?

1. What is a goal that is absolutely 100% attainable this year?
2. What is the goal in between? What goal is just on the edge of what you think you can accomplish, but know you could if you really went for it?
3. Are you holding onto a secret goal? Do you need to incorporate that into the above questions or do you need to readjust and trust your goal?
4. Now that you have the vision, how can you make it more specific?

Step 2: Once you develop your vision you need to figure out what markers need to be achieved along the way. For this step you will define three objectives that must be accomplished in order to reach your destination. In order to define your objectives, write out the answers to the following questions:

1. What skills do you need to work on in order to accomplish your long-term goal?
2. What needs to happen in one week? One month? Six months?
3. How will you know when you have accomplished each objective?
4. Your objectives are the milestones along the path to your destination. Using your answers as a guide, what are the three milestones that will lead you to your destination?

Step 3: The next step in creating your goal plan is to define the strategies you will use to achieve your objectives. For each objective define the what, when, where, and how of each one. Spell out exactly what you will do. The more specific you are the more likely you will be to follow your plan. To help further define your strategies answer the following:

1. What potential obstacles will I face in working on my strategies?
2. How can I address each obstacle?
3. How can I make each strategy more specific?

Step 4: Now it is time to plug it all into your master Goal Plan. Figure out how you want to visually represent your plan. You can go to www.carriecheadle.com to use the Goal Plan template or create your own. You need to write out the plan and then post it where it will be visible on a daily basis. Writing out the goal deepens your connection and ownership of the goal. Having your goals posted helps to serve as a visual reminder and motivator of what you want to accomplish. Remember that goal-setting is a skill. The more you practice it, the easier it will get to answer the questions and create your master Goal Plan.

Tool: Goal Check-in

When you're on a road trip there will be times when you have to change your agenda. You could encounter road blocks, get bad directions, run out of gas, decide to take a cool side trip — it's all part of the journey. Reflecting on the progress of your goals increases your accountability and your motivation. If you don't set aside time to check in on your goal progress, you won't be seeing any progress. This is an important and often neglected step in the process of setting goals. This feedback is imperative if you want to build on your success and be able to see when your goal needs to be adjusted. You need to utilize this tool if you want to be successful with your goal plan.

Step 1: Pick two specific dates to do a mid-goal check-in. Write the dates and time on your calendar for each check-in.

Step 2: Choose a goal buddy. A goal buddy should be someone that will be supportive, but also someone that will keep you accountable. Your goal buddy is not only someone that you can share your goal with, but someone that will check-in periodically and ask you how things are going. You can even send him a copy of your Goal Plan so he can ask you specific questions when you check in.

Step 3: On your check-in dates, take the time to sit down and reflect on how things are going with your goal so far. This will provide you with valuable feedback as well as provide another form of accountability to keep you on track with your goals. Write out your answers to the following:

1. What kind of progress have you made towards your goal so far?
2. What tools or techniques did you find beneficial in helping you work towards your goals?
3. Did you encounter any obstacles? How did you deal with them?
4. Are there any changes or adjustments that need to be made to your goal?

Once you do your check-in you can also touch base with your goal buddy and give him your progress update. Setting goals isn't a one-time deal. Developing your goal plan is a fluid process. As you check in on your goals, you will refine and rewrite your goals. Without this step your performance and grasp of what you are working towards will stagnate. Answering these questions will help you figure out if you are on track or if you need to adjust your goal.

chapter 4

RELAXING THE BODY

"Some of us shake on the outside, some of us on the inside."
—Roberto Clemente, Hall of Fame baseball player

My all-time favorite sport is snowboarding. Every year around the month of October I get excited with the anticipation of the coming snow. I start watching film clips of skiers and snowboarders effortlessly flying down giant bowls of beautiful steep mountains. I can picture myself taking wide sweeping turns down a groomed run or short fast turns in the trees, I can even sense how my body feels as I make each imagined turn. While watching those film clips and seeing myself on the slopes, I can't wait until my board touches the snow that season.

As much as I love to snowboard, my anticipation of snowboarding wasn't always so enjoyable. Some years ago I lived in Lake Tahoe, home to some of the top rated ski resorts in the country. While I lived there I had an unfortunate phenomenon occur every time I drove down the road to my home resort. As soon as I turned left off the highway and started driving the two-mile approach to the slopes, the butterflies would start. They were so intense that I would get sick to my stomach. I was so nervous I would find myself suddenly forgetting to breathe. I was oblivious to everything going on inside the car – conversations, the radio… I was completely consumed with how nervous I was and how awful I felt. I'll spare you the details, but let's just say that the first place I went to when I arrived at the resort wasn't the ski lift. As soon as the car made that left turn I was triggering my stress response. That drive to the resort was *miserable*. So miserable that I started to dread the drive the moment I decided to go snowboarding. In fact, it was so miserable that I would question whether I wanted to go at all.

As you read in the first chapter, one of the problems with the stress response is that it can get triggered during situations when it isn't needed (like driving down the road to a ski resort). You also learned that there is both a physiological and psychological component to that response. Those physiological symptoms of stress and anxiety can be less than optimal for an athlete. Your perception of what is going on physically within your body can have a profound effect on your performance. From the physiological symptoms of nerves, to the searing muscle pain during a hard effort, athletes are constantly navigating the world of their physical bodies. It wasn't until I started my graduate studies in sport psychology and moved away from the snow that I finally started to turn things around. I was learning tools to help athletes perform to their potential and decided I needed to try them out on myself and see if I could get a handle on my nerves. During my next car ride to the ski resort, I used different tools to manage my level of intensity. Some of the tools I used helped me relax my body so that my racing thoughts would follow suit and disappear. Other techniques helped me relax my mind so that my racing heart would calm down. Deliberately relaxing your body can in turn help relax your mind. In this chapter we will focus on the physiological aspects of your stress response and look at how to interpret and manage that physical activation for optimal performance.

Physical Activation of the Body

One of the consequences of experiencing performance anxiety is the effect it has on the athlete's physical body. The body is designed to respond physiologically to a perceived threat to your well-being. As far as your body is concerned, being nervous about an upcoming competition means that there is an impending threat. That's exactly what was happening to me on the road to the ski resort. Being nervous about snowboarding triggered my stress-response getting my body ready to respond to the threat by preparing me to either run or fight for my life. Each time I turned down that road and triggered that response, the reaction was strengthened. My brain and body learned "when we turn down this road, it's time to freak out." To stop that cycle I had to consciously change that response with the tools you will read about in the next four chapters.

Expanding on the concepts from the first chapter of the book, let's revisit the potential physiological symptoms you may experience as a result of performance anxiety:

- Increase in muscle tension
- Decrease in coordination
- Decrease in balance
- Tunnel vision
- Inability to concentrate
- Poor decisions
- Rapid and shallow breathing

- Butterflies or feeling sick to your stomach
- Racing heart
- Difficulty sleeping
- Increased sweating
- Quick to fatigue

As you can imagine, the symptoms of increased muscle tension, inability to concentrate, and being quick to fatigue are going to greatly impact your performance. Your perception of whether or not you find a certain situation stressful will trigger a certain amount of arousal. *Arousal* is a combination of physiological and psychological activation in response to the situation and there are many different factors that can change your level of arousal. Just moving from being inactive to being active, like getting up off the couch and walking outside to get the mail will change your level of intensity. Things that might be thrilling or exciting like riding a roller coaster or watching a scary movie will increase your level of arousal even more. Big life events like graduation or getting a new job can also influence the amount of intensity you feel. And then there are performance situations that may make us feel a little nervous and will increase our arousal, like taking a test or giving a presentation. When you experience performance anxiety it dramatically influences your level of arousal. Standing on the free throw line, getting passed in a race, seeing time ticking down on the clock; if these situations cause you to feel anxious, they will also cause you to increase your level of arousal. Anxiety is an emotion we feel that alerts us of a potential future threat and arousal is the amount of intensity you feel in your body and mind as a result. Any time you feel anxious it will change your level of arousal. The previous list of physiological symptoms is an example of the type of arousal you might experience when your feelings of anxiety elicit your stress-response.

Optimal Zone of Intensity

Another way to think about arousal is to think about it in terms of *intensity*. How much intensity do you need in order to have an optimal performance? Each athlete has his own optimal intensity level that puts him in the right physical and mental space to perform his best. You don't always show up to a day of practice or competition dialed into the exact level of intensity you want. You are often either under or over your optimal level rather than right on target. If you have ever experienced pre-performance anxiety, then you have probably experienced feeling over your optimal zone. If you have ever struggled with your motivation, then you've probably experienced what it's like to be under your zone. There are many different ways to work towards getting yourself into that optimal zone of intensity and this chapter will focus on the physiological factors involved. If you are so lethargic that you can barely move, your level of intensity will be too low to achieve optimal performance. If you are so nervous that your body is shaking and you can't focus, your level will be too high to achieve optimal performance. Somewhere in between is your optimal zone. That optimal zone depends both on the individual and the task involved.

Task Factors

In general, certain sports and certain positions may require different levels of intensity for optimal performance. The optimal zone for the performance situation depends on how complex the task is. The complexity of the task is factored in by the amount of motor and cognitive control needed in order to effectively execute the task. Performance situations that use fine motor skills and require tremendous precision will tend to have a lower zone of intensity for optimal performance. Performance situations that require larger muscle groups or actions using gross motor skills and require less decision making will have a higher zone of intensity for optimal performance. Tasks like putting in golf or a batter about to take a swing will require a lower zone of intensity versus a football player blocking or an athlete sprinting down the field.

Individual Factors

All of that being said, there are also individual differences that influence the optimal zone for an athlete. Two athletes playing the same position in the same sport may require different levels of intensity in order to perform their best. Some athletes are able to tolerate higher levels of intensity than others. Factors like personality and skill ability will influence the amount that is optimal for each person. Some people want to pump themselves up before competition and others try to calm themselves down. This can become challenging when you are on a team and you and your teammates require different zones for optimal performance. Years ago while working with a women's collegiate soccer team, I started doing imagery sessions with the team in the locker room before the games. During the sessions the players would move from visualizing how they wanted to feel as they walked out onto the field to seeing themselves on the pitch feeling strong and confident and having a great performance. Over time, some of the athletes realized that the imagery session wasn't what they needed to get optimally prepared for the game. For some of the athletes it got them too relaxed and for others, just thinking about the game got them too keyed up. Once they all had a chance to try it, we made the sessions optional and about half of the team did the sessions and the other half used different tools to get them into their optimal zone. The optimal zone and path to getting there is specific to the individual. Everyone's optimal zone is different and even if two people have similar zones they may require different tools to get them there.

The Impact of Over-Intensity

The spectrum of intensity goes from lethargic on one end to quadruple latte on the other. When you get nervous before competition, more than likely your intensity level is higher than you need it to be. Tipping the scale to that side leads to a host of issues that will detrimentally impact your performance. Practically every football movie has a scene with two players banging on each other's chests and helmets to get pumped up before heading out onto the field. This can be a problem when one of those players needs to lower his intensity to gain control of his body and get his head in the game. The greatest physiological impacts of over-intensity are the effect it has on your heart rate, breathing, and muscular tension.

Muscular Tension

Your muscular system is made up of hundreds of muscles, tendons, and ligaments that work together to perform multiple roles in the human body. One of the main roles muscles have is to produce all of human movement from creating the expression on your face to doing drills out at practice. Many of those muscles function in groups and work together in order to produce the desired action. When muscles work together this way, the main muscle involved in producing the most force to execute the movement is called the *prime mover* (also known as the *agonist*). One of the other muscles in the group that simultaneously assists the movement is the *antagonist*. Together the prime mover and the antagonist create an *antagonistic pair*. The antagonist muscle is the muscle that opposes the prime mover. For example, the triceps and biceps create an antagonistic pair of muscles and both of those muscles can play either role depending on which muscle is needed the most to produce the desired movement. During the movement, the role of the antagonist muscle is to relax as the prime mover contracts. The antagonist relaxes in order to allow the prime mover to control the movement, but if the antagonist muscle is tense it will impede the movement of the prime mover.

During an athletic performance, if you are over your optimal zone it can create an excess of muscular tension. An excess of muscular tension can cause a breakdown in the execution of a motor skill. For example, imagine contracting all of your muscles and then trying to swing a golf club or a baseball bat. Your movement won't be as fluid when your muscles are overly tense. This is because some muscles need to be relaxed and others contracted in order to properly execute the skill. An increase in muscle tension will also lead to a decrease in coordination and balance. Imagine simultaneously tensing all of the muscles in your body and then trying to do a cartwheel. Even if you can't imagine yourself doing a cartwheel, you can probably feel in your body how the excess muscle tension might get in the way of producing that movement. An additional consequence of muscle tension is that contracted muscles require more energy and oxygen than relaxed muscles. If you are experiencing muscle tension as a result of your nerves, you are using up your body's fuel. It's like having a gas leak in your car. Most of the gas is still going to the engine, but some of it is getting needlessly spilled out along the highway. Coordination, balance, skill execution, and conserving energy are all imperative for athletic performance. Working on relaxation skills will not only help calm the mind, but will help reduce muscular tension that impairs skill execution and contributes to quicker fatigue.

Shallow Breathing

You may have noticed that during times when you feel anxious, you have a tendency to experience shallow breathing or holding your breath.

When you are relaxed, your body reverts to its natural breathing rhythm. This type of breathing is called *diaphragmatic breathing*. Diaphragmatic breathing goes by many names. You may have heard people refer to it as yoga breathing, belly breathing, abdominal breathing, or just relaxed breathing. The diaphragm is the sheet of muscle that lies below the lungs and heart and above the stomach and liver and is the main muscle involved in respiration (i.e. breathing). If you are employing diaphragmatic breathing, when you inhale the diaphragm contracts causing it to flatten and press down moving the organs in the abdominal cavity out of the way to allow room for the lungs to fully expand. Upon exhaling, the diaphragm relaxes causing it to move upward in the shape of a dome, pushing against the lungs to help force the air out of them.

As you learned earlier, one of the symptoms of eliciting your stress response is an increase in muscular tension. When your abdominal muscles are tight they prevent the diaphragm from being able to contract and allow the lungs to fully expand. To test this out, wherever you are right now, tighten your abdominal muscles and then try and take in a deep breath. This time relax your stomach and try again. Notice a difference? When people refer to "belly breathing" you aren't actually breathing with your belly; it is simply that a relaxed belly allows the diaphragm to do its job and without a relaxed belly, you are only breathing with your upper and middle chest. Chest breathing, or shallow breathing, is another symptom of your stress response. In addition to the muscle tension impacting your ability to breathe, some athletes also have a tendency to hold their breath or breathe shallowly when they are feeling anxious or under pressure. Now here's the kicker – not only is shallow breathing a symptom of the stress response, but shallow breathing also causes us to feel more anxious and can trigger the stress response. The ability to control your breath is one of the greatest tools you have for eliciting your relaxation response and managing your nerves.

When I was a kid, my cousins and I spent many summer afternoons in our grandparents' swimming pool. One of our favorite games to play was "Tea Party". The game was simple; we would take in a deep breath and then plunge into the water and sit on the bottom of the pool pretending to have a tea party to see who could stay down at the bottom of the pool the longest. When you breathe there is an exchange of gases occurring between oxygen and carbon dioxide. This exchange not only occurs in the lungs, but in your blood and tissues as well. Remember that there is an ideal state for everything in the body and your body is always trying to get back to homeostasis. As you hold your breath carbon dioxide is building up inside your body and that buildup of carbon dioxide causes your heart rate to increase. Imagine you are sitting at the bottom of the pool holding your breath as you feel your heart beating a little faster. Carbon dioxide build up also causes the levels of carbon dioxide to become too high and affects the pH (level of acidity) of your blood. Your brain responds to the pH imbalance by forcing you to inhale. When holding your breath, you will hit your breaking point and burst through the surface of the water to take in a deep breath, bringing in oxygen and restoring the chemical balance. However, as you sit on the bottom of the pool, your racing heart and the anticipation of needing to take a breath will sometimes cause you to break the surface before your body actually needs to. Inevitably, the game became a competition of both physical and mental endurance.

Not only do the factors of shallow breathing, increased heart rate, and muscular tension impact your performance on a physiological level, they are also often interpreted as negative and further contribute to your feelings of anxiety. Anxiety leads to over-arousal, or too much physiological and psychological activation. Your brain listens to your body and your body listens to your brain so, additionally, when you feel tension in your muscles, your brain can falsely interpret it as a symptom of feeling anxious. If a triathlete is waiting for her swim start and is feeling sick to her stomach in anticipation of the open water swim, her brain is telling her that she is nervous while simultaneously interpreting her physiological symptoms as indicators of feeling nervous, making her feel even more nervous. It takes deliberate work both on the body *and* the mind in order to break this cycle. At the end of the chapter you will get to work on the tool of diaphragmatic breathing. This type of breathing not only reduces your feelings of anxiety by helping to slow down your heart rate, regulate your breathing, and reduce muscle tension, but it also gives you something to focus on. When you are focused on the proper technique of diaphragmatic breathing, there is less room for your brain to focus on your nervous thoughts.

What's my Optimal Zone?

Athletes often have an idea of where they need to be on the spectrum to perform their best and will naturally employ different strategies to get themselves there. However, occasionally where an athlete thinks they should be isn't where they really need to be for optimal performance. In order to figure out where you fit on the spectrum of intensity you can look at the characteristics specific to your sport and position, as well as figuring out what is right for you individually. You can start to assess your optimal zone by asking yourself:

- Does my sport and position require a lot of fine motor skills and precision?
- Does my sport and position require a high amount of quick and complex decision making?

- Think back to some of your other best performances: Were you relaxed and calm? Tense and focused?
- Did you separate yourself from other people and find a quiet space to warm up and prepare on your own without distractions?
- What kind of music were you listening to? Are you choosing music that gets your heart racing and your blood pumping or music that gets you relaxed and focused?
- Did you avoid talking to others so you don't get too worked up before a game?
- Were you talking to people about others things to lighten the mood?

Assessing your optimal zone is the first step, and then accepting your optimal zone is the next step. Sometimes athletes will get wrapped up in what they think they *should* be doing or how they *should* be feeling before their performance. Don't worry about what anyone else is doing and *don't worry about what anyone else is thinking about what you're doing.* Figure out where you need to be on that spectrum in order to have your best performance and trust that. After assessing and accepting, the final step is to learn and implement the tools you need to get to your optimal zone. Several years ago, I was working with an athlete that knew she needed to go off on her own in order to relax and get optimally prepared for competition, but was concerned with what her fans and team would think. She didn't want to hurt anyone's feelings and didn't want to neglect her team. She didn't know how to balance her concern for others while also taking care of herself. Through our work together she was able to recognize what she really needed to do in order to perform her best and we created a plan that allowed her to be with her fans and her team, yet still slip away to give herself the space she needed to get into her optimal zone.

How Do I Get it There?

If you tend to be up towards quadruple latte and your preferred place on the continuum would be somewhere closer toward the middle, the time leading up to competition can be miserable. Luckily, there are techniques you can learn and implement in order to lower your level of intensity and manage the physiological impact of your nerves. Right now, as you read this sentence, take a moment to consciously relax the muscles in your face and in your hands and then take a deep breath. Repeat this phrase: "Relax your hands, relax your face, and breathe." As you did that, what did you notice? What was the first thing that happened after your relaxed your face, hands, and took in a deep breath? For most people, they notice that they automatically drop their shoulders next. For others they notice that for a moment their whole body relaxes. Relaxing your hands and face sends a little message throughout the rest of your body to relax as well. If at that moment your mind was filled with worries and doubts you may have noticed that your thoughts "relaxed" too. Some people even find themselves letting out a nice big sigh in the process. Reducing the amount of physiological tension you are experiencing in your body will help you reduce your feelings of anxiety. Here are some strategies that can help get you into your optimal zone:

Progressive Relaxation

The concept that an anxious mind cannot exist in a relaxed body originally came from Dr. Edmund Jacobson. Dr. Jacobson was a physician who understood that anxiety caused muscle tension in the body and that muscle tension in the body in turn caused a person to increase their feelings of anxiousness. He developed a systematic way of relaxing the body in order to help people relieve a variety of conditions caused by anxiety. The technique was called *progressive relaxation* and helped people reduce the tension in their body and therefore reduce the anxiety they were experiencing. If you have ever been introduced to any relaxation technique, chances are it was born out of Dr. Jacobson's technique of progressive relaxation. The technique has gone through many variations as people have applied it over the years, but the basic technique involves systematically going through the body tensing and relaxing different muscle groups. His basic premise was that anxiety causes muscle tension in the body and a muscle cannot be tense and relaxed at the same time. If you can learn to relax the muscles, you will reduce the tension experienced both in the body and in the mind. Again, imagine trying to work out your life's problems while relaxing in a hot tub or getting a massage. The relaxation of the body also helps quiet the mind.

When you utilize the technique of progressive relaxation you are gaining awareness of the difference between how your muscles feel when they are tense and how they feel when they are relaxed. It is a technique for teaching yourself how to consciously relax your muscles. The more you practice this skill, the more skilled you will become at being able to recognize when you are feeling tension in your body as well as releasing that tension in the moment. As you read before, excessive muscular tension can impair your coordination and balance as well as impede the efficient execution of a motor skill. The ability to relax muscular tension in the moment while performing under pressure is an essential skill for any athlete, and once you become proficient in that skill you will be able to scan your body to check for *and release* unwanted muscular tension. An extensive explanation and step-by-step guide to progressive relaxation is one of the tools provided at the end of the chapter.

Reframe the Butterflies

Typically people don't like how it feels when they experience the feeling of butterflies in their stomach, a racing heart, and shallow breathing. If you interpret those physiological symptoms as "bad" it feeds right into that anxiety loop making you feel even more anxious. Your brain gets message number one, "I do not like how this feels" and message number two, "These physical feelings mean I am anxious." This is how it was for me during that miserable drive to the ski resort. One way to manage how much intensity you feel is by working on your interpretation and perception of what is going on in your body. When you feel those butterflies fluttering and your heart rate increasing, try changing the labels you usually assign to those feelings to something more positive. Instead of using the labels of "bad" and "anxious", imagine that your racing heart and butterflies are just your body's way of getting you ready to perform. Imagine drawing energy from it instead of letting it take energy from you. Try creating new labels with a positive spin like "excited" and "energized". Sometimes this simple reframe is enough to take the edge off your anxiety and get your head in the game.

Body Confidence

One of the first messages you receive letting you know that your competitor is feeling under pressure comes from reading their body language. Start to take notice of how people hold themselves when they are under pressure or feeling nervous. *Then start to take notice of how you hold yourself when you are feeling under pressure or feeling nervous.* Are your shoulders dropped? Are you looking at the ground? Are your hands clenched into fists? Is your jaw tight and your forehead wrinkled? Now think about some of the top athletes in your sport. How do they carry themselves? Oftentimes these athletes convey confidence in their body language even after they have made an error. Your brain will listen to your body, so carrying your body with confidence helps send the message to your brain that you are confident. *Acting as if you are confident helps you move in the direction of actually feeling confident.* Not only are you sending a message to yourself by carrying yourself with confidence, but you are sending a message to your competitors as well. If you see the competition with their shoulders slumped and their heads hung low – what are you thinking about them in that moment? My guess is that you are thinking something along the lines of, "This game is ours. We're in their heads. They've already lost the game." Not only are you thinking that about them, but in that moment you also stand up a little taller and hold your head high because it boosted your own confidence to see them starting to break. And that is *exactly* what they are thinking of you when your shoulders are slumped, your head is hanging low, and you're visibly frustrated and losing your confidence. You give your competitors an edge when your body language says you are feeling the pressure or feeling defeated.

Using Music

Have you ever been driving down the freeway listening to a fast paced song and suddenly realize that you are driving at warp speed? Are there certain songs you listen to that instantly change your mood? Music has the ability to impact our emotional and physiological arousal and your entire mood and energy can change when a particular song comes on. We all have songs we listen to that pull at our heartstrings or put a smile on our faces. Movie producers have been using music to influence the emotional reactions of audiences for decades. This reaction is also true for athletes. Research has shown music to improve athletic performance in many ways, from diverting your attention from fatigue, increasing your physiological arousal, to helping you set your pace; music can have a big impact on performance. In addition, relaxing music has been shown to decrease cortisol levels, which can elicit physical relaxation. Cortisol is one of the hormones released when you activate your "fight-or-flight" response causing increased arousal. Once you figure out where your ideal state of intensity is, be sure you are choosing music that is a reflection of how you want to feel. Pick a few different songs and try listening to them before practice and see what works for you. You may find yourself adding different songs to your playlist depending upon the mood you are in and where you need to be.

The Skill of Relaxation

It should be obvious now that there is a strong physiological reaction that can result from feeling anxious and triggering your stress response. It should also be apparent that experiencing performance anxiety either before or during competition can result in going over your optimal zone and can cause physiological symptoms that are less than ideal for performance. Learning these tools of relaxation is not just about reducing feelings of anxiety so you can feel better. That in itself is certainly a worthy cause for learning these skills, but as an athlete, reducing anxiety can also mean improving physical performance. If you are over your optimal zone of intensity, you are getting in the way of your body's ability to perform. If anxiety leads to a detrimental physiological impact on your performance, then working on relaxation will have a positive physiological impact on your performance.

The tools in this chapter are not tools you try to master in one sitting. Just as a basketball player can't expect to make a free throw in competition if he never practices making free throws outside of competition, if you don't practice the skills of diaphragmatic breathing and progressive relaxation, you can't expect to take a deep breath before a big competition and have it actually reduce the amount of arousal you feel. Working on the skills of relaxed breathing and muscle relaxation helps elicit your relaxation response and if you don't practice using that relaxation response, it can atrophy just like an unused muscle. The relaxation tools will only benefit you in competition if you take the time to build the skill and continue to practice.

Chapter 4: Take-Aways

- Experiencing performance anxiety has a profound impact on an athlete's body, which can be detrimental to performance. Learning tools to help you address the physiological symptoms of anxiety can help reduce both the physiological and psychological aspects of arousal.

- Each athlete has their own optimal zone of intensity at which they perform their best. Different athletes require different levels of intensity for optimal performance.

- Employing diaphragmatic breathing that comes naturally to us while relaxed, is also a skill that can be learned to help us relax. Working on your breathing is the most powerful tool you have to reduce your level of physiological intensity.

- An increase in muscle tension impairs your ability to execute motor skills. Reducing anxiety will contribute to enhancing your physical performance by reducing muscular tension that causes a decrease in coordination and balance.

- Help get yourself into your optimal zone by assessing where you need to be, accepting where you need to be, and then learning and implementing the tools of breathing, muscle relaxation, reframe, body language, and music to help you get to your optimal zone.

Chapter 4: Tools

Tool: Diaphragmatic Breathing

The physiological symptoms of stress and anxiety can be detrimental to your performance. When you start to feel tension and anxiety creeping in, your breathing is often the first thing to go. The ability to control your breathing can be a great ally when dealing with tension and anxiety. Diaphragmatic breathing is the foundation of any relaxation or imagery exercise and is the greatest and most accessible tool for reducing anxiety. This tool is broken into different phases in order to first learn the skill in a relaxed setting and then build on that skill and be able to apply it to your performance. For Phase I, create a successful learning environment by starting in a quiet space with no distractions where you can lie down on your back. I will break down the technique into steps and for each step you will take at least five complete breaths.

Phase I: Lying Down

Step 1: As you are lying down, for the first five deep breaths, just bring your attention to the sound of your breathing and start to slow your breathing down.

Step 2: Now place your hands on your stomach. As you inhale, allow your stomach to expand and fill your hands. As you exhale pull your stomach back towards the ground. Repeat this five times.

Step 3: For this series of five breaths, keep one hand on your stomach and place one hand on your chest over your heart. Inhale and allow your stomach to expand and then feel the air moving into your lungs allowing your chest to rise. At the height of your inhale, pause for a moment and then exhale and feel the air moving out of your lungs and pulling your stomach back towards the ground.

Step 4: For the final series of five breaths you will pull all of the pieces together to complete this diaphragmatic breathing technique. Continue to breathe as you were and this time inhale through your nose and then exhale as if you were blowing air out of a straw.

Phase II: Standing

Step 1: Again choose a calm and quiet space to practice this breathing technique. Stand comfortably in an athletic stance with your legs shoulder width apart and knees softly bent. For the first five deep breaths, just bring your attention to the sound of your breathing and start to slow your breathing down.

Step 2: Now place your hands on your stomach. Allow your stomach to relax as you take in your first deep breath. As you exhale, feel your stomach slightly pull inward away from your hands and then make contact with your hands once again as you inhale. Repeat this five times.

Step 3: For this series of five breaths, allow your stomach to continue to relax and pull back as you breathe. Upon the inhale when your stomach expands into your hands, immediately allow the air to fully expand the lungs as your chest rises. At the height of your inhale let your shoulders rise just a little and pause for a moment. Then exhale letting your shoulders drop and feel the air moving out of your lungs and pulling your stomach back away from your hands.

Step 4: For the final step you will pull all of the pieces together to complete the standing diaphragmatic breathing technique. Continue to breathe as you were and this time inhale through your nose and then exhale as if you were blowing air out of a straw.

Phase III: Practice and Competition

It's one thing to be able to work on this skill when you're nice and relaxed, but it's another thing entirely to be able to do it in a pressure-filled situation. When you become proficient at this skill, you can take one or two deep breaths and immediately affect your level of anxiety. This phase will help you bring the skill into situations where it can have a real impact.

Step 1: Test out your new skill and try it during practice. Pick out three times during practice when it would be good to use this breathing technique.

Step 2: Once you have completed Step 1, take it a step further by pairing your breath with a cue word. Choose a word that expresses the emotion you want to feel at that moment. Take in a deep breath and as you exhale think the word to yourself. Using cue words like "calm", "focus", "control", and "smooth" as you exhale can help make that breath a double whammy for affecting your performance.

Step 3: It's time to take it into competition. Pick out three times during competition when you want to use your breathing. A cyclist might choose to use it on the start line, as they start a steep descent, and as they come into a turn. A baseball player might choose to use it before the game, when they are on deck, and in between pitches. Choose when to use the skill and try it out. The more you practice, the more likely you will be able to call on the skill when you really need it.

Tool: Progressive Relaxation

Anxiety-provoking thoughts can lead to physiological tension, which can then be analyzed and interpreted by the brain to mean that you are feeling anxious. One way to break that negative feedback loop is to help reduce the amount of physiological tension you are experiencing. Progressive relaxation is one of the most widely used and widely researched relaxation techniques. As you read earlier in the chapter, this tool will systematically take you through tensing and relaxing the different muscles groups of your body. As you inhale, you will tense the muscle and hold your breath for a moment, and then as you exhale you will feel yourself relaxing the muscle. As you are learning, don't worry if you have to refer to the instructions here. Pretty soon you will have it memorized and will be able to do it on your own. You can also go to www.carriecheadle.com for more breathing and progressive relaxation resources.

Step 1: Lie down and get as comfortable as you can. You can close your eyes or keep them softly focused on a point in front of you. Start to become aware of your breathing, noticing the sound and quality of your breath. Take five deep breaths, practicing your diaphragmatic breathing. Any thoughts that come into your mind allow them to release with your exhalation and drift away.

Step 2: Go through each muscle group, contracting and relaxing the muscle twice. Remember to inhale and contract the muscle, pause, and then exhale and release the contraction. Inhale, contract, hold, exhale, release. Move slowly through the exercises and relax the muscle even more on the second exhale.

- Scrunch your toes contracting the muscles in the bottom of your feet.
- Flex your feet and contract your shins.
- Point your toes and contract your calf muscles.
- Dig your heels into the ground and contract your hamstrings.
- Tighten the muscles in your quads.
- Squeeze your legs together and contract your inner thighs.
- Tighten the muscles in your glutes.
- Tighten the muscles in your abs.
- Pull your shoulder blades together underneath you and contract your upper back.
- Push your hands into the floor and contract your upper arms.
- Clench your hands into fists and contract your forearms.
- Shrug your shoulders up to your ears and contract your shoulders and neck.
- Slightly clench your teeth tightening the jaw and neck.
- Squint your eyes and wrinkle your nose.

Step 3: Notice any area of your body that is holding extra tension and focus on that part of your body. Use your breath to deeply relax the muscles that are carrying extra tension. Allow yourself to take several deep breaths in this relaxed state. When you are ready to complete the progressive relaxation exercise, you can slowly count from five to one and feel the energy coming back into your body more and more as you count. Move your hands and feet, move the muscles in your face, and bring energy back into your body before you finally open your eyes.

chapter 5

RELAXING THE MIND

"I am an old man and have known a great many troubles,
but most of them never happened."
—Mark Twain

Have you ever been daydreaming and suddenly found yourself laughing out loud or getting a little teary-eyed? Or have you ever started a conversation with someone mid-thought because you already had the beginning of that conversation in your mind? Or how about being so tired that you can't wait to go to bed, but as soon as your head hits the pillow the wheels start turning and you're wide awake? The mind is a powerful force. It can keep you up all night as it fills up with concerns and to-do lists. It can make you feel emotions just by thinking about certain scenarios. It can even have you convinced that you had a conversation with someone even though that conversation only happened in your head. Your mind runs the show and it is doing just that — constantly running. From the multitude of ways to wish for something to come true (wishing wells, shooting stars, and birthday candles) to the stories that were read to us as we drifted off to sleep ("I think I can. I think I can."), since we were children, we have been taught about the power of the mind.

Every day we have a constant inner dialogue running in the background. That dialogue serves many different roles: It provides a sounding board to help you to work out problems and process information; it can also act as judge and jury; it can be your biggest fan or your strongest critic. As you probably know, having *yourself* as a sounding board isn't always effective. Your thoughts play a very big role in whether you feel prepared and confident or worried and apprehensive going into a game or pressure situation. Anxiety is usually associated with negative thoughts. Decrease the anxiety and you'll decrease the negative thoughts. In this chapter we will explore how decreasing the negative thoughts can help decrease the anxiety.

Getting nervous before competition is normal. It's natural to feel excited and anxious in performance situations. There is nothing wrong with feeling some butterflies in your stomach when you're unsure of what to expect or have a competition that's important to you. In those situations, you aren't going to eliminate those butterflies, but you want to be able to contain them so that they are facilitative rather than debilitative to your performance. In the last chapter we focused on the physiological impact of your stress response and introduced tools to help relax the body in order to relax the mind. In this chapter we're working in the opposite direction and exploring how to relax the mind in order to relax the body.

Your thoughts and emotions influence each other in a tangled web and the emotions you feel will influence what you think and in turn, your thoughts will influence the emotions you feel. With every athlete I have ever worked with, from my youngest athletes to my seasoned professionals, at some point we will be working on the thoughts that they are feeding to themselves. Here are some actual words I have heard from multiple athletes:

- I don't belong here.
- I'm never going to get this.
- I'm not going to make it to the end.
- I'm not ready for this.
- What if I fail and disappoint everyone.
- I'm never going to be good enough.
- I'm going to get hurt.
- I'm going to get beat.

People aren't always able to recognize how their thought patterns contribute to their actions and the outcome of their performance. The way that you talk to yourself can produce feelings of anxiety or feelings of confidence. Relaxing the mind is about having more control over the thoughts you feed into your brain and having your thoughts work for you instead of against you.

Are You Feeding the Monster or Feeding the Athlete?

We are always talking to ourselves. "Self-talk" is that inner voice you hear chattering away in your mind. Your self-talk is how you communicate with yourself and if you are an analytical type of person, you may hear that voice A LOT. You may even feel like your inner voice is more like your inner critic, constantly sending negative messages into your brain. There are times when you may not even realize that you are engaging in self-talk, but there isn't a day that goes by without some thought entering your mind. This constant chatter has a big impact on our lived experience. Athletes experiencing constant chatter before a game that whispers to them their biggest doubts and greatest fears undoubtedly see a detrimental affect to their performance. Imagine for a moment that on one shoulder you have a little *monster* that sits and talks about all of your worries, doubts, mistakes, and fears. Now imagine that on your other shoulder you have a little *athlete* that sits and talks about your hopes, dreams, goals, and strengths. You have a little monster on one shoulder and a little athlete on the other; which one are you feeding? Do you spend most of your time feeding the monster or feeding the athlete? *Whichever you choose to feed the most is the one that will become stronger.*

Our thoughts play a part in creating our self-concept — how we carry ourselves and interact with the world around us. When it comes to athletic performance, there are some patterns of thinking that can help your performance and some that can hurt it. Your thoughts have a tremendous influence over your emotions and focus, therefore, self-talk can be as used a tool for getting your emotions and focus where you need them to be for optimal performance. When you're choosing to think instructional or positive thoughts, you're *feeding the athlete*; when your self-talk starts to spiral and you're consumed with negative thoughts, doubts, and worries, you're *feeding the monster.*

Feeding the Monster

In general, there are thoughts and beliefs that are beneficial (positive) to your performance and ones that are detrimental (negative) to your performance. Negative thoughts impact your belief in your ability and your motivation to take the risks necessary to excel at your sport. Those thoughts can keep you stuck in a plateau as you are struck with the fear of failure or fear of success. "I'm never going to be able to stay with these guys to the finish." "How could I have made that mistake; I can't shake it off." "I feel so much pressure to perform now that I'm doing well." When it comes to relaxing the mind, however, it's not as simple as thinking more positively and eliminating your negative thoughts. Negative thoughts can also help you recognize that something needs to change and can even motivate you to make that change. When you are stuck in the thought and are unable to move into action, negative thoughts contribute immensely to your feelings of anxiety and can ruin your performance. Here are some ways that negative thinking and *feeding the monster* can be detrimental to your performance:

Worry: Much of our feelings of worry come from our own inability to tolerate uncertainty. Worry is where the dreaded "what-ifs" reside. What-ifs are the doubts and fears you have about events that *might* happen in the future. These types of worries take you out of the moment and into the future and have you wringing your hands and wondering about what will happen. For example, if you are about to enter your very first triathlon, you might be thinking: "What-if someone swims over me during the swim?" If you are a high school lacrosse player, one of your what-ifs might be: "What-if someone passes to me and I drop the ball?" Worry is not a facilitative type of self-talk to engage in. However, if your worry leads you to prepare for the future and take some action, *then* it becomes beneficial. For example, if you're the triathlete worried about the swim, your worry becomes facilitative if you get a group of friends together so you can practice keeping your cool while they swim all around you. If you're the lacrosse player worried about dropping the ball, your worry becomes facilitative when you decide to meet a teammate thirty minutes before each practice and put in some extra time catching passes. However, most of the time athletes just get stuck in the worry and become overwhelmed and exhausted by it. Worry and what-ifs are ways that we think in worst-case scenarios and feed the monster our doubts and fears.

Judging: Athletes will experience negative self-talk in response to situations when there is a discrepancy between what they want to accomplish and where they are at in the moment. If your performance isn't going the way you had hoped you will often start evaluating and judging your performance. When you start judging and evaluating during your performance, you take your head completely out of the game. You feed the monster when you make judgments about yourself, especially when the judgments you make paint you in a negative light. When things aren't going as planned, you often immediately condemn yourself. You come to the conclusion that there is something wrong with you, that you are having a bad performance and give yourself an automatic sentence of throwing in the towel. Judging yourself against where you thought you would be or comparing yourself against someone else helps feed the monster, compromising your confidence and taking your focus out of the game.

Ruminating: Another way that athletes experience negative thoughts is when they get stuck in a negative feedback loop after making a mistake or having a bad game. A baseball player that dropped the ball in the previous inning is back on the field thinking, "Please don't hit the ball to me." A downhill skier misses a gate and replays it over and over in her mind getting more upset with herself every time and thinks, "I'm so stupid; I totally blew it." When you get stuck in those negative thoughts they can feed into your anxiety and misery. They get carried forward into the next inning or next race and make it more likely that the same thing will happen again. You are so worried about making the same mistake that you can't get out of your head and get back into the game. One of the ways you "feed the monster" is by beating yourself up for making an error or for having a bad race. This kind of negative self-talk can impact your immediate performance as well as your overall confidence. Those thoughts create a story in your mind and when you go into that next inning or next performance, you tell yourself that story again. The story you choose to tell impacts your confidence, motivation, and focus moving forward (more on that in Chapter Eight).

Beliefs: The way we interact with the world around us has to do with our past experiences and what we have come to know as the way the world works. If you believe the world should work a certain way and are then presented with a situation where it doesn't, those thoughts and emotions can rattle you and take your head out of the game. However, sometimes those beliefs aren't accurate and can hold you back from being the athlete you could be. An athlete that has an off-game can move from the *thought* "I had an off-game" and generalize it to the *label* "I am a bad athlete". An athlete that has hit a *plateau* will move into a *slump* when they personalize it by saying, "Why does this have to happen *to me?*" Former professional Brazilian soccer player, Ronaldo Luís Nazário de Lima (generally known as "Ronaldo"), understood this concept when after a World Cup loss he said, "I am still the greatest player in the world. I just didn't perform well that night." Making assumptions that things are working against you, are done to you, or should and shouldn't work a certain way are negative beliefs that produce emotions like anxiety, anger, depression, and guilt, emotions that greatly affect your performance. You are feeding the monster when you get stuck in a belief system that is inaccurate and detrimental to your performance.

Comparing yourself to others: When it comes to sports, athletes often find themselves sizing up the competition to see where they fit in. Comparing yourself to someone else can serve as a source of feedback. It can let you know how you're progressing in your ability and demonstrate what is possible in your sport. However, comparing yourself to others can turn into feeding the monster when you perceive that someone else is better than you; therefore, you're a horrible player, are a complete failure, should quit your sport, etc. This kind of comparison is dangerous to your motivation and confidence. When you gauge your success based on how you did compared to others versus whether or not you are improving in your own performance, it can be harmful to your motivation and stagnate your growth as an athlete. Comparing yourself to others can be a positive source of motivation when you can have respect for someone else's performance and are then inspired to improve your own. If you had a great performance, but still got beat that day, you *feed the athlete* when you say, "I'm disappointed in the outcome, but I had a good performance. I'm ready to readjust my goals to get to the next level." You feed the monster when you think, "I did everything right and I still didn't win. What if I'm never good enough? That guy didn't even deserve to win." When you can respect the sport, respect your competition, and respect yourself – you're feeding the athlete.

Feeding the Athlete

Unfortunately, sometimes the term "positive thinking" gets a bad rap. When some people think of "positive self-talk" it makes them think of the eternal optimist spouting out feel-good statements to make everything and everyone feel better. You imagine they'll say something like, "If you just think positive thoughts, you can make all of your dreams come true!" It's a lovely thought, but positive self-talk is much more than wishful thinking. What *is* true is that what we think influences what we do. *Feeding the athlete* is about deliberately choosing your thoughts to help you move you in the direction you want to go. Having the discipline to work on this part of your performance is one way you can proactively work on the skills of confidence and focus. Here are some deliberate ways to work on feeding the athlete:

Affirmations: Affirmations are like little mission statements. They are sentences or phrases that describe what you want to achieve or how you want to feel as if they are already true. They are powerful messages that can help influence your feelings of competence and confidence. You can create a list of affirmations for different types of situations. For example, I could create affirmations for more general situations, like my role as a Mental Skills Coach or my role as an athlete. I could also create affirmations for specific situations like going into a presentation ("I am confident in my ability and I am a great presenter."), recovering from an injury ("I am getting stronger every day."), or affirmations for a specific event or race ("I am excited and ready to race."). We tend to be very good at creating lists of personal doubts, but struggle when it comes to creating lists of positive affirmations about ourselves. We think they sound hokey or we feel like we don't want to sound boastful, however, creating affirmations will help bring you closer to what you want to accomplish by bringing it into your consciousness and stating it as if it is already true. At the end of the chapter you will have an opportunity to practice feeding the athlete by creating your own list of sport affirmations.

Instructional: Another type of self-talk that can bolster your performance are thoughts that are basically directions for your focus or mood. When learning a new skill we naturally give ourselves instructional cues to help remember what to focus on in order to execute the skill. When you are learning or refining skills, it can be beneficial to deliberately create these cues to help you stay in the moment and not let your brain get overloaded which can affect the execution of the motor skill. Instructional self-talk can also be effective when you are putting out a big effort or when your body is feeling tired. Cues like "power", "energy", and "strong" can help keep you going when your body is screaming for you to quit during a sprint or when you are starting to drag your feet at the end of your game or race. You can also use instructional cues after making a mistake or experiencing a bad call to help control your emotions in the moment. Cues like "let it go", "calm and controlled", or "unstoppable" can help shift your mood, keep your focus in the moment, and your head in the game.

Thinking about what you don't want versus what you do want: Try this exercise. Take a nice big deep breath and clear your mind. Now — don't think about a shark. You can think about anything else, but don't think about a shark. So ... did you think about a shark? When I say, "Don't think about a shark" your brain first has to process what you *don't* want to think about, by thinking about it! As soon as you hear the word "shark" an image pops into your mind of what that means to you. Any thoughts or emotions you have associated with the word are a part of that image as well. You only *stop* thinking about a shark when you give yourself something else to think of. In the context of sport, you are inadvertently feeding the monster when you are thinking about what you *don't* want versus what you *do* want. For example, if before your competition you think to yourself "Don't be nervous" your brain automatically processes "What does it mean to be nervous?" When you say, "Don't be nervous" your brain hears and responds to "nervous" first and "don't be" second. Same with "Don't drop the ball". Your brain first has to process what it means to drop the ball. In a flash you see yourself dropping the ball and the resulting impact and emotions that come with it. Saying *what you want* versus what you don't want is one way to be deliberate about the language you choose to use in order to feed the athlete. Instead of saying, "Don't drop the ball" you say "Catch the ball"; instead of feeding yourself the thought, "Don't be nervous" you reframe it and feed the athlete by saying, "I'm confident and ready".

Happy File: Sometimes you need to help change your mood in order to change your mindset. Influencing how you feel emotionally can influence the thoughts you're having. You are practicing feeding the athlete when you consciously help yourself experience the emotions that are facilitative to your performance. Oftentimes we are trying to change our self-talk to help shift our mood, but there are also ways to help shift your mood to change your outlook. Whenever I am feeding the monster and feeling frustration or doubt about something, I pull out my "Happy File" (yes — sometimes grudgingly). In the file I have collected notes I have received from people over the years sharing how I've helped them or how something I wrote impacted them and reading through the notes helps me to shift my emotional state from feeling frustration and doubt to feeling hopeful and confident. You can create your own version of a "Happy File" by writing out a list of your accomplishments (as you did in Chapter Two), improvements, things you are proud of, nice things people have said about you, etc. Then pull it out and read through it when you need your own confidence booster.

To explore the impact of feeding the monster or feeding the athlete, let's go back and revisit our triathlete and lacrosse player. Our lacrosse player's team is playing in a game against their rival team. She's nervous about the game and wants to do well. During the game she constantly worries about dropping the ball and finds herself creating situations where the ball will be passed to someone else. When she finally does get possession of the ball, she makes a bad pass resulting in a turnover. She berates herself for making the pass and can't let it go. She knows she is a better player than this and can't figure out how to get out of her own way. Overall, her season has been pretty good and she has seen some improvement, but after this one game she feels like her whole season is a failure. She even finds herself wondering if her teammates hate her and if her coach secretly wants her to quit. Every step of the way she is feeding the monster and the monster is getting stronger and stronger with each negative thought, image, and belief she feeds it. Many times, without even realizing it, we engage in self-talk that is destructive to our performance. We unconsciously choose this path because the thought pattern has become habit and we're thinking it before we are even aware of the fact that we are thinking it.

Our triathlete is now about to compete in her second triathlon. In her first race she was able to get through the swim, but she was miserable the whole time. "I was nervous the entire swim. It was awful. The whole time I just couldn't wait to get out of the water and have it over with." She was afraid that she would be the last swimmer out of the water. She was overcome with worries about having so many people around her and getting accidentally hit or kicked in the face. She stopped several times to let other swimmers get around her so she wouldn't have to be near anyone. For her second triathlon she set a goal to improve her swim time and knows that she could easily accomplish her goal by working on managing her pre-race nerves and her fears about the swim. She knows she was feeding the monster during her first triathlon and she is ready to feed the athlete. To help, she wrote a list of affirmations to read the night before and the morning of her race. Her affirmation list said:

"I am a strong swimmer."
"I am confident and relaxed in the water."

"I am smooth and consistent even when people are swimming around me."
"I can handle myself. I'm ready for this."

She knew where her focus needed to be during the swim and came up with her instructional mantra of "relax and breathe". She even created and practiced an imagery script where she visualized people swimming on top of her and all around her and still felt strong, repeating her mantra and keeping her cool. All of her mental preparation helped her to feel more confident and keep her focus on her swim instead of on how nervous she felt. She did her homework and worked hard to feed the athlete and both felt and saw the impact it had on her performance. Through these examples and through your own experience you can see the difference in your outlook and your performance depending on whether you choose to feed the monster or feed the athlete.

Can Negative Thinking Be Positive?

As you can see, there are many different reasons why we engage in negative self-talk. From feeling unprepared, to being frustrated that you aren't on track with your goals, to automatic programming, negative thoughts can be pervasive. There's plenty of research showing that negative self-talk can contribute to your feelings of anxiety and be detrimental to your performance. However, some of you reading this might be thinking that the thoughts you have that other people might define as "negative" don't feel negative to you. For example, if it's raining outside and I feel my motivation to run slipping away from me, the mantra I say to myself is, "I'm not made of sugar!" which loosely translates to "I'm not going to melt in the rain so suck it up and go run!" Some people might argue that there are more positive things I could say to myself in that moment to feel more confident and excited to go run. I could say,

"I am a strong and confident runner no matter what the weather", or "I'm excited for this opportunity to train in the rain", but your self-talk is more powerful when it is personally meaningful to you. Whether your "negative" self-talk is negative depends on your perception of it. When I say, "I'm not made of sugar", it sparks my motivation and reminds me that I'm tough and I can handle a little run in the rain. Another example comes from a cyclist I worked with who was working on his focus and at times would find himself drifting to the back of the pack without even realizing it. He came up with the mantra "How's the view?" which meant if he looked up and saw a sea of butts in spandex, he needed to move up. He could have said to himself "Top ten" to remind himself to stay near the front, or "My head is in the race and I'm focused." There are many options he could have chosen, but "How's the view?" is what he needed in the moment in order to get the job done.

There are also some people whose anxiety is actually relieved by expressing their negative thoughts and going through all of the worst-case scenarios. Expressing their negative thoughts out loud helps them to process and eventually figure out ways to prepare for those worst-case scenarios in order to alleviate their anxiety and manage their nerves. However, this can produce the exact opposite effect in others. Sometimes we are like emotional sponges and take on the emotions of the people around us. You hear a teammate going through the process of expressing his negative thoughts and as his anxiety lessens, yours shoots through the roof. If this rings true for you, you may need to learn the valuable lesson taught to us by a well-known water-loving bird, the duck. Ducks waterproof their top layer of feathers when they preen so that even when they dive under water, their bottom layer of downy feathers will stay completely dry. When you watch a duck dive under the water and resurface, you can see the water beading up and rolling right off of its back. If you tend to soak up the emotions of people around you, you need to waterproof yourself and let those emotions roll off your back to prevent them from influencing you. I've even had athletes put a little yellow rubber duck in their gear bags or lockers to help them remember to not be sponges, soaking up the emotions of the people around them. You need to recognize that *someone else's anxiety is not your anxiety*. On the other hand, if you are the teammate that alleviates anxiety in this way, you need to know that voicing your anxieties and concerns out loud is producing the exact opposite reaction in your teammate. Try to process internally, on paper, or with someone that can handle it and knows how you operate so you can help create the best atmosphere for both you and your teammate. Everyone is different, and one way isn't better than the other. You have to figure out what works for you while at the same time remain open to the fact that other people may need to take a different path to reach the same goal.

Automatic Thought Patterns

Revisiting concepts from the first chapter, you may remember that your thoughts are one of the contributing factors that can elicit your stress response. Negative worries and thoughts can manifest into stressors and trigger your stress response activating an immediate physiological reaction that isn't necessarily beneficial to your performance. A stressor is some sort of demand that you need to respond to. Some examples of demands you face as an athlete are:

- The last batter of the game with two runners on and the score is tied.
- A cyclist trying to bridge up to the break.
- A soccer player taking a penalty kick.
- A triathlete getting in her brick workout in 100° heat.

While these demands are stressors faced by the athlete, whether they are "stressful" has to do with each athlete's perception of whether or not they have what it takes to meet that demand. Part of that appraisal process comes from our feelings of confidence. Are we prepared for the stressor? Have we had success in these types of situations in the past? Additionally, part of that appraisal also comes from your *perception* of your ability, which is influenced by your thoughts in that moment. Your feelings of confidence and your thoughts will impact what you do. This appraisal impacts the decisions that you make and the actions that you take in that moment. Here are some examples of how different appraisals can lead to different outcomes:

Situation: The last batter of the game with two runners on and the score is tied.

Feeding the Monster ...

Appraisal: "It's all coming down to me. What if I choke? I don't know if I can do this."

Emotions: Anxious, intimidated, and uneasy

Performance: Focus is internal, muscles are tight, and the batter strikes out looking.

Feeding the Athlete ...

Appraisal: "One pitch at a time. I can do this."

Emotions: Calm, determined, and confident

Performance: Stays relaxed and focused on what is in his control. Makes a solid hit and brings a runner in to win the game.

Situation: A cyclist trying to bridge up to the break.

Feeding the Monster ...

Appraisal: "I don't know if I have it today. What if I blow up and my race is done?"

Emotions: Unsure, hesitant, and concerned

Performance: Hesitates and misses the opportunity that would have got him in the winning break.

Feeding the Athlete ...

Appraisal: "This is the race right here. I've got it in me. I can do this."

Emotions: Powerful, positive, and hopeful

Performance: Catches the break, recovers, and is able to do the lead out that gets his team the win.

Situation: A soccer player taking a penalty kick.

Feeding the Monster ...

Appraisal: "I've never scored on this goalie. My team is counting on this. What if I miss?"

Emotions: Overwhelmed, scared, and pressured

Performance: The player tenses up, hesitates on the approach, and misses the shot.

Feeding the Athlete ...

Appraisal: "I've made this shot a thousand times in my head. I know I can do this. This goal is mine."

Emotions: Certain, excited, and assured

Performance: She takes in a deep breath, controls her focus, and makes a strong shot on goal.

Situation: A triathlete getting in her brick workout in 100° heat.

Feeding the Monster ...

Appraisal: "It wasn't supposed to be this hot. My body doesn't do well in the heat. This sucks."

Emotions: Miserable, irritated, and stressed

Performance: She is negative the entire time and ends her workout early.

Feeding the Athlete ...

Appraisal: "So what if it's hot, I can handle it. This will be perfect training in case it's hot on race day."

Emotions: Inspired, eager, and capable

Performance: Sticks to her workout plan and feels more confident and prepared about the potential of racing in heat.

Obviously there are many different outcomes that can occur for any given appraisal, but you can start to see the importance of your appraisal when faced with a stressor and how it can impact your performance. The most important aspect of these examples is that the thoughts occurring to the athlete in the moment are part of that appraisal process. Those thoughts let them know how to react in that situation. There are many factors that influence those thoughts originally, but eventually those thoughts can become automatic. Instead of truly processing whether or not you can handle the situation, the thoughts that come to you are what you have created through habit. Some athletes create automatic thought patterns in response to certain situations. For instance, if the soccer player taking a penalty kick has performance anxiety and goes into the situation afraid to miss and questions her ability, then takes the shot and misses, her feedback to herself will be "See, I knew I couldn't do it. I knew I'd screw it up." That feedback loop now continues into the next time she takes a penalty kick. It even continues into the next time someone else takes a penalty kick as she reinforces her position and thinks to herself, "I'm glad that's not me out there." Eventually she creates an automatic "if-then" thought pattern. "*IF* I have to take a penalty kick, *THEN* I will be filled with dread." When you feed that neural pathway long enough, you eventually program yourself to the point that it becomes your default setting. In that situation she will automatically defer to her default setting of not feeling confident when faced with taking a penalty kick.

Your perceptions that lead to your appraisal are not always accurate. Perceptions are fluid and can change as you get new information and have new experiences. There are situations when your appraisal has become an automatic thought pattern versus an accurate assessment of the situation. The good news is you can change those automatic thought patterns; you can go in and rewrite the program and adjust your setting. You can move from immediately feeding the monster ("This is a disaster."), to feeding the athlete ("I can handle this."). Part of adjusting the setting is paying attention to the language that you choose when making those appraisals. Creating a new neural pathway takes deliberate work. The tools at the end of this chapter will help you to relax the mind and feed the athlete in order to adjust those settings and even create a new default setting that is more facilitative to your performance.

Instructions for Feeding the Athlete

If you have a lifetime of thinking a certain way, you aren't going to change that pattern of thinking overnight. Feeding the athlete takes discipline and practice. There are several steps involved when it comes to choosing more facilitative self-talk and even after you've taken those steps, it still takes a lot of practice. If you have the tendency to be a negative thinker or worrier, it's unrealistic to think that you could eliminate those thoughts entirely. But, feeding the athlete is not about eliminating them; it's about recognizing them and balancing them out.

Before you can begin to change the dialogue that is occurring in your mind you have to be able to recognize when it is happening and catch yourself in the moment. To start recognizing it in the moment, reflect back on your past performances and ask yourself, "During what parts of my performance do I tend to feed the monster?" What thoughts are going through your mind at that moment? Reflecting back on times when you are feeding the monster and knowing exactly what you are saying to yourself in those moments is a great first step to building awareness. Athletes will often say to me, "I don't know what happened. One minute I was doing fine and the next minute I wasn't." Building awareness helps you recognize the process of how your thoughts affect your performance. Once you are able to recognize it in the moment, you need to be able to stop yourself. Recognize that the thought you are having is detrimental to your performance and that you are in control of what you choose to think. Once you become aware, then it's time to feed the athlete. Ask yourself; what do I need to say in that moment to remain calm, confident, and step up to the challenge?

If you have built up a strong neural pathway of negative thinking in certain situations it can feel downright impossible to start feeding the athlete right away. When athletes immediately try to suddenly replace negative thoughts with positive ones they often feel like they are "lying" to themselves and will say to me, "I'm saying 'I'm a strong and confident player', but I don't believe it." Sometimes you need an intermediate step to just move you in that direction, to move just one step away from the monster and one step closer to the athlete. You need to begin to poking holes in the monster's theories and planting the seeds of doubt in the monster's mind. You need to develop another voice; see that there are other options and know that the way you are thinking about the situation is not the only way to think about it. The tools at the end of the chapter will help you to boost your confidence and reduce your anxiety by helping you to work on relaxing the mind and feeding the athlete.

Chapter 5: Take-Aways

- It's not realistic to eliminate all negative thoughts. Just start by working towards spending less time feeding the monster and more time feeding the athlete.
- Not all negative thoughts are negative. Your perception of the meaning behind your thoughts is just as impactful as what you actually say.
- Your thoughts and emotions will affect your performance. If you find that they tend to have a negative influence, it's time to reprogram your automatic thought patterns.
- Working on feeding the athlete doesn't happen overnight. It takes deliberate and consistent effort to choose thoughts that are more facilitative to your performance.
- You can help reduce your feelings of pressure and anxiety by becoming more aware of the piece you contribute through your thought pattern. Are you choosing to feed the monster or feed the athlete?

Chapter 5: Tools

Tool: Sport Affirmations

For most of us, we are much better at creating lists of our fears and doubts than we are at creating lists that build us up. Our thoughts can have a tremendous influence over our global feelings of confidence. For this exercise you will create a list of positive affirmations for your sport performance.

Step 1: Grab a piece of paper and start to brainstorm your list. Think about the doubts you have about yourself and imagine what you need to hear in that moment to boost your confidence.

Step 2: Refine your list. Craft at least eight powerful and positive sport affirmations. Rewrite your list and post it up. Have your list somewhere easily accessible and where you will see it. You might have one taped up in your room and one written on a 3x5 card in your gym bag.

Step 3: Use your list to boost your confidence and feed the athlete. Try the additional suggestions below:

- Read your list before every practice and competition.
- Pick a week to read and say your affirmations to yourself at least five times throughout the day. The more you say them, the more comfortable you become with saying them (and believing them!). I know this is true for my own affirmations "I am calm and confident" and "I am excited and ready for this."
- Choose an affirmation of the day. Choose one affirmation off your list; memorize it and find ways to use it and live by it throughout that day. Rotate through all of the affirmations on your list.
- Say your affirmations out loud. Choose one of your affirmations and start by whispering it. Then say your affirmation a little louder and a little louder until you yell it at the top of your lungs. Don't knock it 'til you try it. It might feel weird or awkward at first to say them out loud, but it can be a very powerful exercise (and it's kind of fun when you get to yell them at the top of your lungs!).

Tool: Changing Your Self-Talk

In certain high pressure or stressful situations it can be much easier to feed the monster than it is to feed the athlete. When you are used to feeding the monster in certain situations, it is going to take some deliberate work to rewrite that script. When those types of thoughts have become automatic, you have to choose *ahead of time* what you need to say to yourself in that moment, otherwise you will defer to your default setting of feeding the monster. For this exercise you are going to practice changing your self-talk from feeding the monster to feeding the athlete.

Step 1: Think about a specific situation when you are likely to lose your confidence or focus. On a piece of paper, describe the situation during which you are likely you "feed the monster" and engage in negative self-talk.

Step 2: What are the negative thoughts you feed the monster in that situation? Come up with two or three examples of exact statements you are thinking in that moment.

Step 3: Read through your negative statements and write down the emotions and feelings that go along with those statements.

Step 4: It's time to work on feeding the athlete. What are two or three positive thoughts you can choose to replace your negative ones? What do you need to say to yourself in the moment in order to feed the athlete? Remember to use the same principles you used in writing your affirmations to create powerful and impactful statements. If you have trouble thinking of something, try this: Think about an athlete that exudes confidence. Someone you look up to and admire. Imagine that they are faced with the same situation; what thoughts would they say to themselves in that moment to remain calm, confident, and in control?

Step 5: Read through your positive statements and write down the emotions and feelings that go along with those statements.

Step 6: Put it into practice. The next time you are faced with that situation – practice feeding the athlete. You can do this exercise for every situation that negatively affects your level of confidence.

chapter 6

CHOOSING YOUR FOCUS

"Concentration is the secret of strength."
—Ralph Waldo Emerson

I've always loved exploring "unchartered territory". My excursions may not have officially qualified as "unchartered", but if it was new to me and it felt adventurous, I was 100% on board. When I found myself on a rock-climbing trip to Joshua Tree National Park and my husband's cousin wanted to lead us on a nighttime adventure through the "Chasm of Doom", I was up for the challenge. The rules were as follows: Flashlights were allowed on the hike out from our campsite, but once we got to our destination, no flashlights allowed and *no turning back*. The Chasm is basically a labyrinth of climbing, squeezing, and tunneling your way through a giant pile of classic Joshua Tree rock. You are constantly communicating with the person in front of you and behind you, trying to navigate your way in total darkness. At one point during our journey, we climbed out on top of a giant boulder into the night air and I clearly remember standing up there and relishing the sweet moment of adventure I was having. Little did I know that sweet feeling was about to change dramatically.

I walked across the top of the boulder to join my friends as our unsolicited guide explained to our group what was next. As he spoke, I found myself staring down into a dark crevasse and immediately felt my heart making contact with my chest. In order for us to continue our journey out of the Chasm of Doom and cross over to the other side of the crevasse we were going to have to stem. This meant securing my right foot on one wall and reaching my left foot across the gaping crevasse to the other wall and then moving forward until the gap narrowed enough that I could climb over to the other side. I started to get down into the crevasse to make my way through and I froze. Panic had set in and my entire focus shifted and all I could think about was how far down it was to the bottom. I felt like gravity was grabbing my ankles and pulling me down into the darkness below. When my husband's cousin started talking me through and telling me exactly what to do, I was finally able to make my first move. He helped me shift my focus from the abyss below to my technique on the rock.

***

The ability to focus is just as integral to athletic performance as it is to stepping over a gaping crevasse. Choosing to focus on things that are in your control and on cues that are relevant to your performance takes discipline and practice. It is intimately connected to your motivation, goals, and confidence. Focus has a hand in every part of your performance. From being able to keep your eyes on the prize and hold onto the big picture to being able to let go of everything else going on and tuning into the moment, focus has a big role to play in your performance. This chapter will help you learn the skills involved in choosing to focus on tasks and emotions that are facilitative rather than debilitative to your performance. The skill of being able to shift my focus, from my fear to my technique (while keeping myself in the moment and tuned into what *was* in my control) were imperative for successfully navigating my way through the Chasm of Doom.

The ability to focus means keeping your mind occupied with the task at hand. Part of the skill of focus has to do with discipline. There is a tremendous amount of discipline necessary when it comes to being a competitive athlete. You have to be disciplined about your nutrition, getting in your training, and getting enough sleep … you also need to be disciplined about where you choose to focus. We spend a lot of time focusing on things that are of no benefit to us. We choose to let ourselves be distracted. We pay more attention to the things that worry us and detract from our confidence than we do to the things that empower us and feed our confidence. We focus on the abyss instead of the rock. When consumed with performance anxiety, it can be hard to comprehend that you are making a choice. Breaking that cycle of feeding the monster and choosing to feed the athlete has to do with *where you choose to focus* as well. How you decide what to focus on is not as straightforward as you might think. There are many factors that influence both your ability to focus and where you choose to direct your focus, and it all starts with the basics of how you process information.

Information Processing

Your senses of sight, hearing, smell, taste, and touch allow you to take in information so you can process it and decide what to do about it. Humans are constantly taking in information from their environment, processing that information, and then making decisions and acting on that information. When it comes to sport, sometimes you know exactly what you need to pay attention to (you're waiting for the sound of the starting gun, you're watching the trajectory of the ball, etc.) and other times you have to select what to pay attention to among a fast moving and ever-changing environment. I'm sure you've heard the example of how your brain is like a computer; information goes into the computer, the computer processes the information, and then it produces a response — input, process, output. When it comes to humans, the act of processing information is broken down into those same three stages. In the initial stage you are receiving information and you need to single out the stimulus. During this time you are basically trying to figure out what input needs to be processed. What do you need to pay attention to? Once you have identified the stimulus you move to the next stage where you analyze the information and choose how to respond. This is where the information is processed and decisions are made based on the cues you have chosen to pay attention to. Once you have made your decision, it's time to move to the final stage, which entails taking action on your chosen response; in other words, it's time to react. It is through these three stages that input is converted to output. The speed at which you are able to go through this process is basically a measurement of your reaction time — a key measurement when it comes to athletic performance. On a very basic level, there are things that can interfere with your ability to focus your attention where you need to because of a breakdown during information processing. Here are some examples:

Too many choices: A huge part of an athlete's ability to focus has to do with knowing which cues are relevant and which ones are irrelevant to his performance. Part of choosing the stimulus is deciding what to pay attention to and what to ignore. When you eliminate options (or distractions) you can make your decision more quickly. For example, if you go to a restaurant that has a five page menu, you will make your decision of what to order more quickly if you go in knowing that you will only choose a vegetarian entrée or you will only choose an entrée from page three of the menu. You allow yourself to NOT pay attention to those things that waste your time and get in the way of making a quick and accurate decision. In sport, you are often faced with a constantly changing environment and you must quickly discern between relevant and irrelevant cues. If you are a baseball player up at the plate, focusing on your last at bat, the other team's screaming fans, and the butterflies in your stomach, then you are focusing on cues that are irrelevant to the task at hand. The more options you have to choose from, the longer it will take for you to decide what you need to pay attention to. Choose the wrong thing to focus on and you've slowed down your reaction time and possibly missed a key opportunity. One way to improve your ability to focus (staying in the moment and reduce reaction time) is to eliminate the number of options you have to choose from.

Limited capacity: Your brain has a limited capacity for focus. It is only capable of processing one or two pieces of information at one time. When you're processing two pieces of information at once, there is less brain activity allocated to each one. The more you have to pay attention to, the less you can focus on each task. You've probably experienced the phenomenon of trying to focus on too many things at once while learning a new skill and having it result in complete information overload. One of the factors that will influence your ability to process information has to do with whether you are a novice or expert at the skill you are trying to execute. When you are an expert at a skill, there are aspects of the skill that become automatic and require less of your processing capacity. Think back to when you were learning how to drive a car. When you were first learning your brain had to spend energy focusing on things like how much pressure to apply to the pedals and how far to turn the steering wheel in order to initiate the turn. Once you're an expert at driving, those actions become automatic so you're able to execute those tasks without having to spend brainpower focusing on them. However, the only way to get to that point is through many hours of practice. If you are learning or refining a skill in sport, you may struggle with focus when your brain is trying to process too much information at one time. When you're feeling overwhelmed and thinking about too many things at once it can produce anxiety, which exacerbates your inability to choose your focus. If you find yourself in this position, you need to stop, take a deep breath, and choose ONE thing to focus on. Or try and switch to how you want the execution of the skill to feel versus focusing on what you are supposed to do. Since you have a limited capacity, where you choose to focus becomes extremely important in terms of performance.

Anxiety and Stress: An additional factor that influences your ability to process information is whether or not you are under stress. A certain amount of anxiety can help keep you sharp and tune in your focus, but too much anxiety and your attention is preoccupied with your worrisome thoughts and racing heart. When you are feeling performance anxiety you are much more likely to be distracted and tune into irrelevant cues. This distraction can impact how quickly you're able to make decisions and your ability to see and capitalize on alternative options. Your anxiety eventually becomes overwhelming and can lead to a complete breakdown in your performance. There's a reason why the chapter on *Relaxing the Body* comes before the chapter on *Choosing Your Focus*. Where you choose to focus can contribute to feelings of anxiety and feelings of anxiety can contribute to inappropriate focus.

When you experience the emotion of anxiety, it will increase your level of arousal and high levels of arousal can lead to a narrowing of focus. In some situations this can be beneficial to your performance because it allows you to give your attentional energy to what is most important at that moment. However, when your arousal passes that optimal point, that narrowing can be detrimental to your performance. For example, during my adventures in the Chasm of Doom, my level of arousal was so high that my attention was completely zeroed in on one thing; how far was the drop below me and was I going to fall in it? My focus was completely internal and it took some time before I could shift it to where it needed to be.

Shifting Your Focus

Take a minute to think about how many times your focus has to shift from the moment your performance starts to the moment it ends; how many shifts actually occur? Did you stop counting? The ability to shift focus is an essential mental skill for an athlete. Sometimes when it appears that an athlete is having a lapse in focus, it's not that he isn't paying attention, it's that he's paying attention to the wrong thing. We are always paying attention to something; it just might not be the "something" that we should be paying attention to in that moment. During the Chasm of Doom I was intensely focused on my fear and how far down the ground was below, which isn't where my focus needed to be at that moment to be able to stem across and get to the other side.

Different types of focus are needed during different points in athletic performance. There are times when focus needs to be broad, allowing you to take in multiple streams of information and other times when focus needs to be narrow and zoned in on one specific thing. Additionally, there are times when focus needs to be external and times when it needs to be internal. You might need an internal type of focus when you are taking in feedback or reflecting on and analyzing your performance. Conversely, your focus needs to be external when you are executing a play or responding to an opponent. The problem is that your focus isn't always where it needs to be when it needs to be there. When I was standing on top of the crevasse in the Chasm of Doom, my focus was internal, totally consumed with my fear, instead of external on where I needed to place my hands and feet. You need to know where your focus needs to be (internal, external, broad, narrow) and how you're going to get it there. The quality of your practice and performance is directly related to your ability to shift your focus.

Dealing with Distractions

The greatest opposition to focus comes in the form of distractions. There are two different types of distractions, internal distractions and external distractions. *Internal distractions* usually take the form of thoughts, worries, and doubts. You might be thinking about the error you made in the last inning or about how you performed against this team before or performed in this event last season. You're worrying about whether or not you will beat your time or win the game. You could be thinking about a fight you had with a friend or about an upcoming exam or interview. You might be distracted by some lingering emotion; feeling upset or angry about a bad call or some piece of feedback you got from your coach. It might be the end of the game and you are tuned into how exhausted you feel. There are any number of internal distractions that can take your focus away from your actual performance in the moment.

The second type of distraction is external. *External distractions* will take the form of things that are outside of you that are irrelevant to your performance. You could be visually distracted by something in your environment. Your eyes could be glued to your heart rate monitor or to the recruiters you know are watching from the stands. You could be distracted by sounds you hear like the cheers or boos of the crowd, the trash talk of the opposing team, or the jeers and air horns of the fans. What is important to note is that these things aren't *pulling* your focus towards them; you are *pushing* your focus to them. If you are choosing to focus on cues that are irrelevant to your performance, you are distracted. Your attention isn't where it needs to be in that moment and you will make errors and miss opportunities as a result. Here are some major distractors that can take your head out of the game and impact your performance:

Fighting against the present: One major contributor to a loss of focus is what I call "butting heads" with the present. Sometimes you get so caught up in not wanting things to be the way they are that it can be difficult to shift your focus back to where it needs to be. The key word here is *acceptance*. For some sports, weather becomes a major player during a competition. Weather is a factor that is out of your control. There is no amount of crying or complaining that will actually change the heat index, how hard the wind is blowing, or the inches of rain or snow accumulating on the ground. Regardless of this fact, athletes will still fight against it. "Yes, I understand that it's raining/hot/windy, *but I don't want it to be.*" They "butt heads" with the weather instead of accepting it and moving on. Until you accept it, your focus won't be where it actually needs to be. Yes, you would *prefer* that it wasn't raining/hot/windy, but it is — so get over it. Accept and adapt. You can even butt heads and fight against what you are feeling in the moment. "I don't want to be nervous", keeps your focus on how nervous you actually feel. *Accept* that you are feeling nervous and you can then shift your focus to something else. "It's OK if I feel nervous. It's natural to feel nervous because I am excited and anticipating the start of the game. My body is just getting ready to play."

Once you've accepted it you can shift your focus to something else that is in your control.

Focus on the outcome: A special distraction that you've probably encountered at some point in your athletic life is when you are focused on the outcome of the game. When you're thinking about whether or not you are going to win or lose, accomplish or not accomplish your personal record, you're distracted by the outcome of your performance instead of focused on the process of what you need to do *right now* to respond to the current situation. One of the most difficult concepts to understand and accept is that when you *let go* of the outcome and focus on the things you need to do to perform your best, you're more likely to get the outcome you want. Yes — it's OK to want to win; however, *wanting to win* and allowing your desire *not to lose* to become a distraction are two very different things. When you're faced with a setback during competition and you're focused on the outcome, in that moment you become consumed with the feeling that your race or game is slipping away. If, when faced with a setback during competition you keep your focus in the moment, you are able to assess and adjust in order to continue to perform your best and keep moving towards you goal.

Getting consumed by your emotions: Your emotions magnify your thoughts and sometimes once you feel the power of that emotion it can *become* you. In his book *Emotional Intelligence: Why It Can Matter More Than IQ*, Daniel Goleman, describes this process as an "emotional hijacking". Emotional hijacking is where you're so consumed by the emotion that it's hard to break away from it. This can be especially true if something goes against your expectations, feels unjust, or you feel like you have no control. When something happens to you, your brain is trying to figure out what category to put it in. It scans all of your experiences and memories and asks, "How am I supposed to feel about this situation?" Once you have chosen a category, your brain sends out an immediate message to activate the chosen emotion and sometimes those chosen emotions can be detrimental to your performance. For example, say that during a game you feel like a call was made unfairly against you and that call has had a significant impact on the game. You are overwhelmed with anger and can't shake how upset you feel. It would be easy to point fingers at the referee, but *your emotion* is what is taking your focus out of the game. Once you start to feel the emotion, your brain gets more signals feeding into that emotion. "I'm angry and this is how I am supposed to react and feel when I am angry." Your brain is hijacked by the emotion and you are finding it difficult to separate yourself from the emotion and get your head back into the game.

Focus on past mistakes: Focusing on errors you made in the past, whether it was in the last inning, your last competition, or last year — it can become a major distraction that takes your focus away from the present moment. When you are "stuck" in the past thinking about an error you made, the distraction comes from the fear of not wanting to repeat it, or being upset with yourself because it happened in the first place. You have to first accept that mistakes are going to be made. I have yet to have an athlete raise his or her hand during one of my workshops when I ask, "Who in here has never made a mistake?" Accepting your mistakes is part of working on the skill of coming back after making a mistake. Beating yourself up and being afraid of a repeat performance are not mandatory responses to making a mistake. If you tend to be the type of athlete that gets angry or upset with yourself after making an error, and then you carry it with you throughout the rest of your performance, you need to make some changes to your operating manual and choose another response that will be more beneficial to your performance.

Focusing on the pain: All athletes know that there will be times when they have to suffer through a hard intense effort in their sport. Your legs are burning, your lungs are on fire, and you can't possibly keep going, but you do. During these intense efforts, the physical pain you are feeling can become a distraction. I'm not talking about the pain of an injury — that kind of pain you need to pay attention to. I'm talking about the pain of effort; the physical discomfort involved in putting out a maximum effort. When you are working out at a high intensity, it can be hard to think about anything else but the amount of pain you're in. As soon as you start thinking about how much pain you're in — that's ALL you can think about. Your mind is now tuned into the pain. Your awareness is super-focused on everything you're feeling in your body and suddenly the pain is magnified. At this point, if you start to panic a little ("I'm burning all of my matches. This hurts too much. I don't think I can keep going."), and elicit your stress-response — the feeling of pain intensifies even more. Our full experience of pain is connected to our perception of the pain. If you decide the pain is awful and bordering on unbearable, your experience and tolerance will be different than if your perception of it is more positive. Staying relaxed and keeping your mind occupied with performance related cues could help you keep your head in the game when your body wishes the game was over.

These examples demonstrate that many times those distractions, the things you get hooked by, are things that are completely out of your control. When your focus is stuck on things that are out of your control, you are burning matches and giving your power away. You end up spending precious energy directing your thoughts and emotions around something that you can do nothing about. You might not have control over the situations that arise and the challenges you meet, but you do have control over your attitude about them and your reaction to them. You can work on the skill of focus by both eliminating distractions and by deciding how you will react to them in order to maintain your confidence and composure in that moment.

Improving Your Ability to Focus

The 1986 film *Hoosiers* (a great film to add to your Inspirational Movie list!) follows the trials of a small town high school basketball team during their journey through their 1952 season. There is a poignant scene when the team arrives at the venue where they'll be playing in the championship game. The team walks into the gym of the opposing team and they're immediately awestruck by the size of the stadium. Anticipating their reaction, the coach asks a player to hold one end of a tape measure so they can measure the distance from the backboard to the free throw line. He then has the players measure the distance of the rim to the floor. He turns to the team to tell them what they already know; that they are the exact same measurements as their court back home. The coach helped relieve their anxiety by helping them to shift their focus from something out of their control to something in their control. He helped them see that there were more things that were the same than were different about the championship game they would play. He eliminated the distraction of the giant stadium and helped them shift their focus to where it needed to be to maintain their confidence and keep their heads in the game. Here are some ways that you can work on your own focusing skills:

Simulation Training

In some ways you can never simulate competition in training because there is a certain amount of energy and intensity that occurs in competition that is hard to replicate during practice. Additionally, you can't pick out and train for every possible scenario that may arise during competition. That being said, ideally you don't want the first time you experience something to happen in competition when you could have prepared for it in your training. There are ways to train with the typical stressors and distractions you will face in competition so you can get used to them and eliminate them as stressors and distractions in your performance. For example, if your rival team usually has a chant or song you hear when you compete against them you can record their chant during a game and have it playing in the background during practice. You can practice regrouping after making an error or having a time out called when you are about to perform. You can also take opportunities to practice in the conditions you will be competing in. For example, if you're a cyclist or triathlete, practice time trialing into the wind. If you're a soccer player, practice your ball handling when the field is wet. You get better at what you practice. Think about ways you can create competition situations during your practice and training.

Mindfulness

One of the greatest challenges for humans is to stay present because our thoughts and energy are often hanging out in the past or projecting into the future. Additionally, so many different things vie for our attention that it takes deliberate effort to truly keep focused in the moment. When many people think of mindfulness they think of the ability to stay present and pay attention to what they are actually doing in the present moment. How often during your day are you actually giving 100% attention to what you are doing right then? Like the Zen proverb says, "When walking, walk. When eating, eat." When you are thinking about a mistake you made or worried about your team's performance and wondering if you are going to pull out the win — you are hanging out in places that don't exist. The past and future don't exist, but your thoughts and energy have a tendency to want to hang out there. One of the greatest things you can do for your athletic performance is to practice this skill of mindfulness. Practice being in the moment versus letting your thoughts and energy "time travel" into the past or the future. True mindfulness encompasses even more than just keeping your focus on the task at hand. It also means the ability to keep your focus in the moment while not judging the experience. As soon as you start judging, you open yourself up to self-talk and emotions that can distract you from keeping your focus in the present moment. Mindfulness also encompasses the ability to free yourself from your emotions. You are not at the mercy of your emotions. Instead of reacting to the emotion, you can step back and accept it in a non-judgmental way. Your emotion is neither good nor bad; it is just how you are feeling at that moment.

Focus Cues

Focus cues are little triggers that help you to bring all of your energy into the present moment or help shift your focus to where it needs to be. Focus cues can be verbal, visual, or physical. Verbal cues are similar to what you read about in the last chapter on informational self-talk. These types of cues are words or short phrases that help keep your focus where it needs to be in that moment. Visual and physical cues can help when you need to shift your focus from internal to external. A visual cue is something external that can serve as a refocusing trigger. A cyclist might tape a verbal cue to her handlebars, a football player might write it on his shoe, etc. A physical cue can be something you do that triggers the time to focus or refocus. Two little jumps to get ready for action, wiping your hands down your legs to forget the past play, putting on your helmet, etc. The most important part of using these cues is *intention*. When you say the word or perform the motion, you are doing so with the intent of harnessing your focus and shifting it to where you need it to be.

Performance Routines

With many sports there are breaks in performance when your mind will tend to wander. A performance routine can help you keep your attention where it needs to be when it needs to be there. Performance routines can help you refocus and they can also help you to keep your focus where it needs to be when you are performing under pressure. An outfielder might have a routine before each pitch. A basketball player might have a routine before a free throw. A soccer played can develop a routine before taking a penalty kick. You can also create a post-error routine to mentally recover from your mistakes and move forward. Pulling up a few blades of grass and dropping them behind you, dragging your foot in an arch in front of you as if you are wiping something away, taking a deep breath and reciting your refocusing cue while you exhale, these are all deliberate routines created to regain composure and shift your focus back to where it needs to be.

Time to Choose Your Focus

When you are under stress, you are more likely to be distracted by factors that are irrelevant to your performance. When it comes to focus and performance anxiety, people tend to go internal when they need to be external. You are in your head, which is filled with worries and doubts and feeding the monster, instead of externally focused on what's happening in the race or game. This is the type of focus that can start the creation of a slump. A batter steps up to the plate and desperately thinks, "Don't strike out looking." Her focus is up in her head instead of on her performance. She's missing the external cues she needs to read in order to execute the skill and she strikes out looking. She creates the circumstance to bring to fruition the thing she fears the most. The second time that she strikes out looking is a slippery slope — but what started it was not having her focus where it needed to be. She was being controlled by fear instead of choosing her focus.

Your ability to manage your anxiety and relax your body will impact your ability to focus. Where you choose to focus can contribute to an increase or decrease in your level of anxiety and confidence in your ability. The thoughts you feed yourself can influence where you focus and where you choose to focus can influence the thoughts you feed yourself. Your ability to set effective goals can help harness your focus and your ability to focus can help you with your motivation to improve and desire to set goals. Working on one area will help support another area and vice versa. All of the concepts and techniques in this book support each other and are interconnected in their impact on your performance. The tools at the end of this chapter will help you define where your focus needs to be and help you learn how to get it there.

Chapter 6: Take-Aways

- Conserve your mental and emotional energy and help eliminate distracting factors by choosing to focus on the things that are in your control.
- Focus is an essential mental skill for successful athletic performance. It takes discipline to choose to focus on the things that are facilitative rather than debilitative to your performance.

- Don't fight against what's happening in the moment. The quicker you accept it, the quicker you can shift your focus to something that is in your control.
- Where you choose to focus can contribute to your anxiety and anxiety can contribute to an inability to choose appropriate focus. Work on both ends.
- You get better at what you practice. Take opportunities to simulate competition situations during training and practice.

Chapter 6: Tools

Tool: In/Out of Control

Many times the things that hook you and end up distracting you from keeping your focus where it needs to be are things that are out of your control. Defining the factors that are both in your control and out of your control can help eliminate distractors and keep your focus where it needs to be.

Step 1: Grab a piece of paper and draw a line down the middle of the page, creating two columns. One column is titled *In Control* and the other is called *Out of Control*.

Step 2: Think about an upcoming competition. On your paper you will start to brainstorm all of the things that are in your control and out of your control when it comes to your performance. Think of all of the factors that could affect your performance as well as the outcome of the competition and plug them in to the column where they belong. If there are any factors you feel cross the line between in and out of your control, try to be specific and define what aspects of it are out of your control and what aspects of it are in your control.

Step 3: How do you want to use your list? Set up a time to revisit your list before your competition to help remind yourself to keep your focus on the things that are in your control.

Tool: Critical Moments

In every sport, there are times during your performance when it becomes imperative that you are optimally aware and focused. In the book *The Mental Game Plan: Getting Psyched for Sport*[3] the authors called these times "critical moments." Some of these moments are unique to the sport and some are unique to you. Defining your critical moments helps you create an optimal focus plan for your competition. (Remember you can go to www.carriecheadle.com for worksheets and examples.)

Step 1: Define the critical moments of your performance. From the moment your competition starts to the moment it ends — what are those key points in time when you need to have optimal focus to get through that moment successfully? Grab a piece of paper and make three columns. In the first column you will write out each of these moments. This defines WHEN you need to have optimal focus.

Step 2: In the second column, for each critical moment, you will define WHERE your focus needs to be in order for you to perform your best in that moment.

Step 3: Now that you know WHEN the critical moment is and WHERE your focus needs to be, you need to figure out WHAT you're going to do to get it there. In the third column, write down what visual, verbal, or physical cue you will use in order to get your focus where it needs to be when it needs to be there.

Step 4: Continue this process for each critical moment of your performance. Once you are done you will have created your optimal focus plan for competition. Just writing out your plan can help you eliminate focusing on distractors and help you to remember to keep your focus on what is in your control.

chapter 7

PREPARATION = CONFIDENCE

"How many successful people have you ever heard say, 'I just make it up as I go along' I can't think of one."
—Mike Ditka

Every year from January to mid-March an elite squad shows up in El Centro, California, to begin their training. The intense effort they exert during training is paramount because during their performance there is no room for error. This elite squad is made up of active duty Navy and Marine Corps and together they make up the team members of the Blue Angels. Every year the Blue Angels fly in shows around the country performing "The Demo"; an aerobatic demonstration of both solo and group flight maneuvers. But before they can fly in the first show of the season, they must endure intense training to prepare. Every morning of winter training starts with a pre-dawn briefing followed by a mental rehearsal visualizing that day's flight. Their mental preparation is exact because their maneuvers have to be exact.

The Blue Angels are famous for flying in The Diamond, which is a formation created by four jets that fly in a tight diamond shape. In order to fly that close to each other and be safe, they can't fly while looking straight ahead. They have to fly while looking at a spot on the jet next to them which they call "flying paint". (Look over your right shoulder and imagine that you are flying a plane straight, but have to keep your eyes trained to your right. Now reach your right arm out and imagine that there is a blue and yellow F/A-18 Hornet flying at your fingertips. At times, the amount of air that separates the jets from each other is *less* than that distance.) They practice The Diamond formation until they are eventually flying at speeds up to 400mph and eighteen inches apart. You have to have tremendous trust in yourself and in your team in order to fly that close at those speeds and then execute The Diamond Roll, a 360-degree roll performed as one unit. 400mph. Eighteen inches. No room for error. The intensity of their preparation and training has to match the amount of confidence they must have in their ability to safely execute the maneuvers and put on a flawless show.

When you get to the moments before your competition begins and know that you've done everything you could to set yourself up to be successful on that day, you will go into your event with the same amount of confidence as the Blue Angels. When you feel *prepared* to face the challenge in front of you, you feel more confident in your ability to do so. As an athlete you are constantly faced with making choices that will enable you to be either more or less prepared for optimal competitive performance. From whether or not you are getting in all of your training hours, to the quality of your practice, the type of fuel you are putting in your body, to the amount of sleep you're getting, and whether or not you are taking time off for your physical and mental health — on game day your choices around these factors surround you and influence how confident you feel. If you want to feel confident in your ability to rise to the challenge and conquer the competition, you need to be willing to make the sacrifices it takes to prepare both mentally and physically.

There is a misconception that athletes on top of their game are always confident. They exude confidence; they wake up feeling like warriors and go to bed feeling like champions. But confidence isn't something that you are; it's something that you do. Confidence comes from the thousands of hours working on your physical skills and then dotting all the i's and crossing all the t's of your mental game. It comes from knowing you have done everything in your power to be prepared and put yourself in the best position to have a successful performance.

Why is Preparation Important?

This might seem like a ridiculous question, but why is preparation important? What is the point of preparing yourself for game day? It's a more complicated question than you might think. There are many different phases of preparation, from the choices you make in the off-season all the way up to the choices you make in the hours leading up to your performance. A more important question might be; *why do people sometimes choose not to prepare?* The decisions you make about your preparation are established by what you expect to get out of it. When you are faced with a choice to make, you will go through a process of evaluating:

1. Will this actually improve my performance?
2. How important is it to me right now to improve my performance?

Your *honest* assessment of these two questions determines what you decide to do (and what you decide not to do) in preparation for your event. When faced with that choice, if you call into question the value of the act and estimate that the potential impact to your performance is not that great, you may choose not to do it. If you believe that the consequences of your actions won't have a significant impact on your performance, then why do them? You might think to yourself, "Sure, it would be good to do 'X', but I don't really think it's going to make a difference so I'm not going to do it." If you don't see any reason to improve your performance, then you also might not be motivated enough to make the choice to do something to prepare for your performance. You might think to yourself, "I could do 'X' and it would probably help my performance, but I'm burned out on my team and burned out on this season and I don't care how I do." You may not even be aware that you are going through this process as you make these decisions, but you weigh the investment against the reward. If, in your mind you don't calculate a reward, you don't make the investment. When you do decide, yes — I value the outcome of this performance and yes — I think accomplishing this action would improve my performance, then you will make the choice to take that action in order to prepare. This is exactly what happened for me when I finally turned things around and got a handle on my nerves before going snowboarding. I was ready to change how I felt and I was introduced to some tools I could use to decrease my anxiety and increase my confidence. My performance was important to me and I believed the investment would produce the desired result so I chose to prepare.

Preparation doesn't just occur right before your event. At any point before your game or race you can ask yourself — how confident do I feel right now in my ability to accomplish my goal? Then on a scale from 1 – 10 (1 meaning you have absolutely *no confidence* and 10 meaning you have absolutely *no question*), where do you rank yourself? Now ask yourself, with the time you have left before game day and with what is in your control, what can you do to improve your confidence by one point? Or even by a half point? Here are some examples:

Baseball Player

Time: Off-Season

Goal: Win a starting position and help team win the state championship

Confidence Score: 5

Increase Score: I would move from a five to a six if I showed up to the first day of practice feeling strong.

Mountain Biker

Time: Week Before a Race

Goal: Top 10

Confidence Score: 7

Increase Score: I would move from a seven to an eight if I could find a trail with some roots to do laps on.

You'll be amazed at how much control you have and how taking control of your actions and preparation can lead you to feel more confident. Once you define what it is that will help improve your confidence, you can turn it into a specific goal following the guidelines from Chapter Three. By assessing your confidence and figuring out how to increase your score you are taking charge of your preparation. Taking this step demonstrates how confidence is something that you do. Don't worry about moving to the top of the scale. Confidence can come one point at a time and just focusing on that one point can help you choose to do something that is in your control. That one point gives you something tangible to work on to prepare for your event, improving confidence, and alleviating performance anxiety.

Pre-Performance Anxiety

In the first chapter we explored general situations that can lead to feelings of anxiety:

- The outcome is important to you
- The situation is new and you don't know what to expect
- Things are unpredictable
- You feel like you have no control
- Fear of failure
- You are experiencing life stress

There isn't an athlete in the world that hasn't felt nervous before a performance. No matter what the cause, the result of how anxiety affects you is usually the same. The good news is, that sometimes those nerves dissipate over time, once you gain confidence and experience in your sport, and then you may only feel those nerves before bigger events. When talking about pre-performance anxiety there are some specific situations and scenarios that can contribute to feeling those butterflies. Here are some additional sport- specific situations that can lead you to feel some anxiety leading up to your performance:

Pressure to perform: Some athletes feel mounting pressure as they get closer and closer to game time. It's as if someone started blowing up a balloon the day before the game and continued until moments before the start of your competition. They keep blowing and blowing and the balloon gets bigger and bigger until it feels like the balloon is about to burst. Without the tools to manage those feelings of anxiety, and letting some air out of the balloon, that's exactly what will happen; the balloon will burst. The amazing thing I have found is that much of the pressure put onto athletes is pressure they put onto themselves. Even when you are feeling pressure from someone else to perform, you then take that feeling, turn it inward, and *own* it. You take their expectations in as pressure. (Other people's expectations go on the "Out of Control" side of the list.) And sometimes there are other emotions and agendas that get tangled up with your sport and get transferred into pressure to perform well:

- You're coming off a bad performance and don't want to let your teammates down
- You've had a rough couple games and you're afraid your coach is going to take away your starting position
- There are recruiters/family/friends coming to watch the game
- You've spent a lot of time away from your family and friends in order to train for this event

All of these scenarios get transferred into pressure to perform. More than anything you want to put your best foot forward and perform well, but the amount of pressure you are putting on yourself is undermining your performance.

Expecting to be nervous: Your expectations influence your beliefs and vice versa. Your expectations of feeling nervous lead you to believe that you will feel nervous. Your belief that you will do well leads you to expect to do well. These expectations and beliefs affect your level of confidence going into your event. When you want to see how you should feel about the future, you compare it to how you felt about that situation in the past. If you are chronically anxious before competition, you're sending a strong message to your brain and body about how you should feel in anticipation of your next event. Think about when you trigger your alarm; when is that first moment before a competition that you start to feel the butterflies fluttering around? Some athletes sound the alarm the moment they start thinking about their event and for others it gets triggered closer to the event, the night before or the morning of. These feelings of anxiety will be even stronger if you have any association of a past poor performance going into your next one. Not only are you anticipating feeling nervous, you are also experiencing negative feelings about not wanting to have a repeat bad performance, which can intensify your feelings of anxiety.

Mislabeling your nerves: Athletes can become nervous before their competitions because they have simply mislabeled the physiological symptoms of their stress response. That response is there for a reason. Activating the stress response sets things in motion to help you prepare to perform. However, for many athletes, that physiological response happens to be followed by feelings of anxiety and so the two get paired together. As soon as your heart starts racing, you immediately think, "Oh man, I'm nervous". You decide that those feelings are bad so you label them "bad" and therefore create your path:

"The road is made by people walking on it, things are so because they are called so. What makes them so? Making them so makes them so. What makes them not so? Making them not so makes them not so." Chuang-tzu

As you learned in Chapter Four, you need to reframe the thoughts that coincide with your heart beating faster and the other physiological symptoms you feel. You need to tell yourself that this is how your body is preparing you to be ready to battle. It's honing your focus, increasing your heart rate, and pumping blood into your muscles to get your body ready to move. Those feelings are only "bad" if you call them bad. You "make it so" or "make it not so" by what you choose to call it.

Comparing yourself to others: One sure way to set yourself up to feed the monster and induce anxiety is by comparing yourself to others. It's natural to compare yourself to others in your sport. Comparing yourself to the competition provides you with a gauge of what is possible, where you stand, and what you need to do if you want to reach the next level. However, a problem occurs if you compare yourself to those people and then experience an immediate hit to your confidence. Your feelings of confidence in your ability shouldn't change depending on who is on the start line or whom you are playing against that day. (Your competition also goes on the "Out of Control" side of the list.) You have no control over who shows up and how much they have prepared for their own performances. What you need to focus on in order to have your best performance stays the same no matter who shows up to compete that day.

Haven't mentally prepared for the time leading up to competition: The final reason that you could be experiencing anxiety before your performance is that you simply haven't put any thought into your mental preparation leading up to your event. You don't have a pre-performance plan in place that has been deliberately created and refined to choose your thoughts and focus before your performance. You might think that your performance starts when the whistle blows, the gun goes off, or the ball drops — but your performance actually starts when you start prepping for your event. How you approach the time leading up to your event has everything to do with how you perform. At the end of the chapter you will have the opportunity to create your own pre-performance plan to help you prepare optimally for your performance.

Seeing is Believing

One of your greatest sources of confidence comes from knowing you have dealt with this situation successfully in the past. Human evolution has given us a tremendous gift in the form of your pre-frontal cortex, which gives you the ability to plan. With this ability and the help of additional parts of your brain, you can create images of things you have never previously experienced. For example, you don't actually have to make anchovy-flavored ice cream and then taste it to know it will taste bad. You have the ability to imagine the future *and* the ability to change your expectations of that future. An additional resource you have available to you for optimally preparing for performance is the use of *visualization*. Also known as imagery, mental rehearsal, or mental practice; visualization is the ability to see and direct mental images in your mind. It is an essential mental skill utilized by many athletes as part of their preparation for performance. You can either *create* an image (e.g. see yourself executing a move or performing a skill, visualize yourself recovering from an error, etc.) or you can *re-create* an image by visualizing a past experience (e.g. play back one of your best performances, etc.). One of the visualization exercises I do with my athletes is to create a visualization script for a skill they are working on, but don't quite have yet. Together we will create a script that visualizes them expertly executing the skill they are working on. Once we have the script dialed in I will record it so they can listen to it on a regular basis and constantly see those positive images in their minds. For athletes that put an extraordinary amount of pressure on themselves and get nervous before an event, we might work on a script that visualizes one of their best performances to help remind them that they are capable of feeling calm, focused, and in control. By using visualization and creating or re-creating these positive images you can strengthen the desired response when you practice that response in your mind.

With the aid of new technology and brain imaging, we know that visual imagery and visual perception share some of the same neural pathways. What this means is that some of the same pathways are used when someone performs a skill and when someone *imagines* performing a skill.

Basically, the brain is using the same preparatory pathways, but during visualization the actual execution of the motor skill is blocked. When you use visualization to see yourself hitting your free throw, sinking a putt, making contact with the ball, or recovering from an error, you are strengthening the same neural pathway as if you were *actually executing that skill*. Visualization can help performance, however you must be proficient at the skill of deliberately creating and re-creating images in your mind for it to have a positive impact. Your ability to see vivid images and be able to control those images is part of that skill. If you can't control the images in your mind and can't see them clearly, then using visualization can actually be detrimental to your performance. You don't want to build up the neural pathway that has the response of you filled with panic when you step up to the free throw line or line up for your race!

If you want to become more skilled in using visualization, like anything else, it takes practice. There are some important principles to keep in mind when you're starting out: Choose a quiet place to practice visualization where you won't be disturbed and get yourself relaxed. Start your visualization practice by beginning with your diaphragmatic breathing to help quiet your mind. Once you improve your skills you'll be able to visualize wherever you are in the moment, but choosing a quiet setting and getting relaxed will allow you to be successful when learning and practicing the skill. Since part of the skill of visualization comes from the ability to create a vivid image in your mind, you need to practice that as well. You can make the images in your visualization vivid by incorporating your five senses of sight, touch, smell, hearing, and taste into the script. Imagining how the bat feels in your hands, the smell of the pool as you step onto the starting block, the sound of the gun at the start of your race provides details that sharpen the images in your visualization. The other essential skill involved with visualization is the ability to control the images in your mind. If you find that controlling the images is challenging, start off by practicing with something that is familiar. It could be seeing yourself brush your teeth, visualizing your bedroom, eating your favorite food, etc. Really get into the details and remember to incorporate your senses. You can practice the skill with things that are familiar to you and work up towards using visualization in sport specific situations. Here are some ways to use imagery in order to prepare for optimal performance:

Visualization Exercise: Seeing Past Success

In this exercise you create a script of one of your best performances and spend time visualizing that performance. If you did the exercise at the end of Chapter One you can revisit your Peak Performance Vision and refine it to create a visualization script. Choose a performance when you felt strong, confident, and focused. Put pen to paper and actually write out your script remembering to incorporate your five senses. Once you have your script, you can memorize it or even record yourself or a friend reading it so you can just listen to it. Use this visualization exercise to boost your confidence and help get you into your optimal emotional state as you see and feel yourself performing at your best.

Visualization Exercise: Skill Execution

During the Blue Angels winter training, the pilots never sat in the pilot's seat without first visualizing the exact maneuvers they were going to perform that day. In this exercise you can use visualization to see yourself executing a specific skill. It might be a new skill you're working on, or a skill you are trying to make adjustments to. If you're having trouble seeing yourself perform the skill in your mind, you can try filming yourself successfully performing the skill and then practice your visualization immediately after watching yourself on film. Try changing the perspective by going through the visualization once as if you were watching yourself on video and then try it again as if you were in your body and seeing it through your own eyes.

Visualization Exercise: Emotion Control

This exercise can help you seamlessly regroup and refocus in the face of a challenge or setback. Think about a situation that would typically throw you off your game. Write a script that demonstrates you keeping your cool and handling the situation with your confidence and focus intact. Because your mind is so powerful, sometimes just thinking of these scenarios can produce feelings of anxiety. If you find that doing this visualization exercise gets you so worked up that you can't control the images, try starting with the Plan B tool at the end of Chapter Nine and then revisit this visualization exercise again and see if you are more able to control the images and see yourself executing emotion control.

Getting Mentally Ready to Perform

Using visualization can give you the opportunity to mentally rehearse how you want to feel and what you want to do during your performance. As you get closer to game time, there are specific things you can do to make the mental shift from "game off" to "game on". At times there will be things occurring both inside and outside of your sport that try to pull your energy away from your performance as you push your thoughts toward them. Many of the tools and techniques in the chapters on *Relaxing the Body* and *Relaxing the Mind* help you learn how to prevent automatically eliciting your stress response and learn how to manage the physiological and psychological symptoms when you do. There are other ways to create outlets and performance routines to help you deal with both on-the-field and off-the-field distractions to your performance.

Being able to compartmentalize thoughts and worries can relieve anxiety and help you refocus when you find yourself distracted by things that you are powerless to do anything about. Some of those thoughts and worries are just pesky what-if's invading your brain and sucking your energy and others are actual worries that you can attend to at another time. Imagine that each day of your life you have a sum total of one dollar to spend on your worries and each worry costs you one quarter. If each time you worried about something you knew you had to give up a quarter, you would think a little harder about which worries were actually worth worrying about. Sometimes you just need to acknowledge that it's something you need to address, but now is not the time. Other times you need to decide if it's actually worth spending your precious energy worrying about. Here are some tools that can help when you are in a situation where you need to put other thoughts and worries aside so you can focus on your performance:

Crossing the Threshold: A threshold is usually a door or entrance that separates one space from another and when you "cross the threshold" you are transitioning, shifting from one existence to another. For example, when you wake up in the morning and walk through your bedroom door you cross the threshold and transition into the start of your day. Before a competition, *crossing the threshold* means choosing a symbolic way to signify that you are ready to perform and helps you transition into competition mode. A Viking putting on their chainmail armor, the war haka performed by the Maori, the war paint applied by a native tribe, these are all symbolic rituals that were created and performed to prepare for the transition into battle. Examples of "thresholds" you could use to make the mental transition into your performance are:

- The moment you step out of the car or step onto of the bus
- Walking out of the locker room
- Stepping onto the court or field
- As you put on some piece of your equipment (tie your shoes, put on your helmet, put on your gloves, etc.)

You can also cross the threshold after your performance. If you are playing in a tournament or racing in a stage race, you might need to create a bookend from one performance to the next. Creating a place to cross the threshold can help you let go of your last performance and make the transition into getting yourself optimally prepared for the next one.

The power that comes from crossing the threshold comes from the intent. You can't just go through the motions. As you cross, you are leaving all other thoughts and worries behind and shifting to game time. All of your energy and resources are focused on what is needed to accomplish your performance goals. You can also think of crossing the threshold as the moment you "become" the uncompromising athlete. Like a stage actor putting on the costume of his or her character, you can cross the threshold and take on the persona of the confident athlete making the shift to performance mode.

Park it: For this exercise you get to use your imagination. There are times during practice or competition when you find yourself distracted by other things that are going on in your life. Your body is there, but your mind is somewhere else. You need to find a place to "park" whatever worries and concerns you have that are occupying your energy so you can shift your focus to where it needs to be in that moment. Here are some examples of different symbolic ways to "park" your thoughts:

- Send them to the basement: Imagine that you are standing in front of an elevator and as the door opens you load all of your worries onto the elevator and then send them down and "park" them in the basement.
- Blow them into a balloon: Imagine that you are blowing all of your distracting thoughts into a balloon. "Park" your thoughts in the balloon by tying it closed and then letting it go.
- Lock them up: Imagine that in your hands you are holding a little black box with a lock. Put all of your thoughts and worries into the box and lock them up. Then imagine putting the box into your locker, the trunk of your car, or some other enclosed space where they will be "parked" until the end of your game.

Shred it: This technique requires a prop. On a piece of paper, write down all of the things that are weighing on you and having an impact on your confidence, motivation, and focus going into your performance. Let it all out and don't censor yourself. Then take your paper and put it through a paper shredder. As you feed your worries into the shredder, actually feel yourself letting them go. Feel yourself let them go as you simultaneously feel yourself bringing all of your energy into the present moment and solely focused on your performance.

Worry stone: Worry stones and worry beads have been used throughout centuries in many different cultures. A worry stone is a small polished stone that you can hold in the palm of your hand and when you rub the smooth cool surface between your fingers, it helps you to feel calm. Hold your worry stone in your hand while you hold in your mind whatever worries or thoughts you have that are keeping you from staying in the present moment. Then take in a deep breath as you rub the surface of the stone and when you exhale, imagine that you are transferring those thoughts and worries into the stone. Even if you don't have a worry stone to hold in your hand, you can visualize going through these same actions in your mind and still achieve the calm you need to let it go and focus on the moment.

———

When you choose one of these ways to let go of your distracting thoughts and worries and transition into performance mode, you are choosing a symbol and assigning an important meaning to that symbol. Whether it's in your mind, like the balloon or the box, or it's tangible, like the paper shredder or the worry stone, that chosen symbol becomes a powerful representation of letting go and getting ready to perform. You can try them all and see which one is the most effective and feels right to you. You can even come up with your own. Which one you choose doesn't matter, what does matter is that once you use it, you use it consistently. When you do this, the symbol becomes so powerful that just thinking about it can help you achieve the same centering result.

Working on Your Pre-Performance Plan

For many athletes, the breakdown in their performance happens before their game or race even begins. Those days and hours leading up to your performance are critical times that often get overlooked. Many athletes just "do their thing" before their competitions without giving any real thought to whether or not "their thing" is actually setting them up to perform to their potential.

If you are serious about performing consistently, you need to be serious about preparing consistently. Being deliberate about your preparation means making choices that will put you in the best position both mentally and physically to be ready to compete. Preparation means covering all areas that can influence the outcome of your performance that are within your control. You need to be physically prepared in order to be on the same playing field as your competition and you need to be mentally prepared if you want to excel on that field. Are you willing to commit to the kind of preparation it takes to feel 100% ready to perform? Spending time preparing for your event and creating your own pre performance plan will help you feel more in control of your confidence and focus going into competition.

Chapter 7: Take-Aways

- Preparation equals confidence because confidence isn't something that you are; it's something that you do.
- If your performance is important to you and you believe that an investment in preparation will actually improve your performance, you will be more motivated to take action.
- Use visualization to practice seeing yourself competing with focused confidence and expertly executing the skills of your performance.
- Get mentally ready to "go to battle" by choosing a symbolic way to cross the threshold and make the transition into game time.
- Take the time to dial in your pre-performance plan and make sure you are making choices that help set you up to perform consistently and perform to your potential.

Chapter 7: Tools

Tool: Visualization Scripts

Visualization is a powerful mental skill for creating images in your mind that you want to execute in life. Being able to see these things in your mind helps bring you one step closer to believing that you can make it happen.

Step 1: Go back and read through the three visualization exercises of Seeing Past Success, Skill Execution, and Emotion Control and choose which script you would like to create.

Step 2: Grab a piece of paper and at the top, write out a general description of the situation and choose a starting and ending point for your visualization.

Step 3: Below your description, list the five senses of *sight, touch, smell, hearing*, and *taste*. Next °to each one, brainstorm ideas of how you can incorporate the five senses into your image. Get creative and think through the images that really bring that scenario to life.

Step 4: Below your senses brainstorm, write out a 2nd list using the words *physical, mental*, and *emotional*. Next to each one of those, write out how you want to be feeling in your scenario.

Step 5: Now it's time to write your whole script. From the starting point to the end, write out what you are doing in each moment of your scenario and be sure to include the key descriptive elements from your visualization brainstorm.

Step 6: Once your script is complete, read it out loud or have someone read it to you. Taking this step will help you see if there are any additions or changes you need to make.

Step 7: Record your visualization using a voice recorder or voice memo software on your computer or smartphone. In the beginning, it's easier to perform the visualization by just listening to the script. Once the visualization becomes strong, you won't necessarily need to listen to it in order to create the images in your mind. When you record it, be sure to talk slow and take a nice long pause between sentences to give yourself time to create the images in your mind as you listen to it.

Tool: Pre-Performance Plan

It's time to set yourself up for success and perform consistently by preparing consistently. This tool helps you create your ideal pre-performance plan (PPP) addressing all of the essential elements for optimal focus and confidence heading into your performance. You'll create a timeline and figure out during each moment what you need to be doing, your ideal emotional state, and your ideal self-talk leading up to game time.

Step 1: Grab a piece of paper and brainstorm all of the things you need to do in the week leading up to your event in order to be prepared. What do you need to do to be mentally and physically ready to go?

Step 2: Figure out your pre-performance timeline by creating blocks of time leading up to your event. For example, your timeline might include the day before, night before, morning of, warm up, and game time. Look over your brainstorm and figure out what blocks of time will logically fit into your PPP.

Step 3: Start plugging the items from your brainstorm into your timeline. From packing, sleeping, fueling, and warm-up to visualization, music, and crossing the threshold — what are all of the elements you need in order to be mentally and physically prepared and where do they fit in your timeline? For now, have a sheet or half sheet of paper dedicated to each block of time for this first draft of your PPP. For each block you will have a place to write out what you need to be "doing", "feeling", and "thinking" during that time leading up to your performance.

Step 4: Now that you know what you are doing — it's time to take it one step further: for each block, identify how you *ideally* want to be "feeling" during that time. Is it confident and calm? Excited and aggressive? What is ideal for you? Write out how you want to be feeling underneath the "doing" section. Don't worry if there is overlap, your ideal emotional state may be the same for some blocks of time. Once you identify how you want to feel, take a look through what you are doing during that block of time and be sure that part of your mental preparation has to do with helping you achieve that ideal emotional state.

Step 5: For this step you will identify your ideal self-talk. For each block, what do you need to be thinking in order to help achieve how you want to be feeling? If you want to feel calm and confident, your self-talk might include "I'm prepared and ready to go." Underneath the "feeling" section, write out your ideal self-talk in the "thinking" section.

Step 6: Once you have all of the blocks written out, pull them all together into one document. Each block of time includes exactly what you need to do, feel, and think leading up to your event. This is your Pre-Performance Plan. Right now, your plan is a work in progress. You will create your plan, test it out, make adjustments, rewrite the plan, and do this until it's dialed in. Make adjustments as needed, but once you have a plan that gets you in the right mental and physical space to perform, use it consistently.

chapter 8

REFLECTION & FEEDBACK

"Tomorrow hopes we have learned something from yesterday."
—John Wayne

One of the first books I ever read that involved the concepts of sport psychology was a book called *Inner Skiing*[4], by W. Timothy Gallwey and Robert Kriegel. One of the aspects of the book that truly stuck with me is that your ability to learn and improve is directly related to the feedback you receive. After reading that book I knew that part of my job would be to help athletes be open to receiving that feedback. You may remember from Chapter Three that one of the greatest pitfalls of setting effective goals is neglecting to get feedback. However, for some people, as soon as they hear that word they think, "Oh no, here it comes" and are filled with a sense of dread. Those people are *certain* that they're about to hear all of the things they're doing wrong, that "feedback" really means, "Here is a list of the ways you are failing." For many athletes, taking in feedback can be extremely uncomfortable and anxiety-provoking. They equate feedback with errors and mistakes instead of progress and improvement. If this applies to you, it's time to change your definition of "feedback".

Think back to the first time you ever participated in your sport. Have your skills improved at all since that day? You have interpreted, integrated, and acted on thousands of pieces of information to get where you are up to this point. All learning and improvement comes from your ability to recognize and act on feedback. Feedback is information about the progress of your performance. It provides you with valuable information for making adjustments, *if* you are open to receiving that feedback. If you want to improve your skills and enjoy your sport, not only do you need to be open to feedback, you need to be proactive about getting it. Here are some types of feedback that can help shape and improve performance:

Outcome: One obvious type of feedback comes in the form of seeing the results or outcome of your performance. For example, if your goal is to sink a putt and you accomplish that, you are getting feedback informing you that the choices you made and technique you used helped you accomplish that goal. If your goal is to hit a grounder between second and third and you pop up, you are getting feedback informing you that the choices you made and technique you used didn't work. Seeing the results of your actions is a source of feedback because it lets you know whether or not your actions were successful. For example, when I'm snowboarding and I find that I'm having a hard time initiating a turn and getting my snowboard to respond quickly, I'm getting outcome feedback that lets me know that I am either feeling anxious or I'm feeling tired and I'm not shifting my weight over my board where it needs to be in order to make the turn.

Performance: This type of feedback is related to the quality of your performance. It may come intrinsically, from your own kinesthetic awareness, or it may come from sources outside of you, such as your coach, a teammate, watching video, etc. Kinesthetic awareness has to do with your ability to feel how your body moves through space. This type of sensory information gives you feedback on whether or not the movement you are trying to execute "feels" right. Feedback related to the execution of a skill can also come from a coach or teammate. This type of feedback adds information you may not be able to feel or see on your own that aids in helping you successfully execute the skill. You can also receive performance feedback by watching your performance on video. You may be able to see how the correct movement is supposed to look or see the faults of your technique you weren't able to feel in the moment.

Rewards and Punishments: Rewards and punishments are used both deliberately and inadvertently to shape your performance. They are a type of feedback that attempts to either reinforce a desired behavior or to change an undesired behavior. Getting a medal or trophy, getting positive comments from a teammate or coach — these are rewards that let you know your performance is going well. Conversely, getting yelled at or being put on the bench might be seen as punishments letting you know that things aren't going so well.

Feedback basically answers the question, "How am I doing?" It provides you with information you can use to continue to improve your performance if you choose to act on it. You can receive feedback both during and after your performance. Feedback during your performance allows you to make changes that could impact your technique and the execution of motor skills. Feedback after a performance allows you to reflect on your performance and evaluate changes to be made or things that should remain the same in order to impact future outcomes.

Why is it Hard to Hear Feedback?

Even though feedback is necessary to accomplish your athletic goals, there are times when it can be difficult to take in feedback. Instead of taking it in as feedback, you hear it as criticism. This selective hearing will prevent you from being able to get information about your performance progress so you can capitalize on that information and advance your skills. Your awareness is impaired because your defenses are up preventing you from seeing or hearing the feedback coming to you. Here are some factors that can cause you to be unable to receive feedback:

Distortion: When you are in a slump and frustrated with your performance, feedback can sound like a reinforcement of how horrible you're doing. You currently feel bad about your performance and your confidence is low so you selectively hear the "bad" in the feedback being given. Instead of being able to listen and hear the feedback, you are overwhelmed with your own frustration and think "Yeah, I know I suck right now and I don't need to hear it from you." You can't receive accurate feedback because your own negative filters are distorting it and that filter is getting in the way of getting the information you need to improve your performance. You need to be able to decipher *what happened* versus *how you feel about what happened.* Your feelings about your performance are clouding your view and keeping you from seeing the positive and constructive aspects as well as the aspects you need to take responsibility for, in order to turn things around.

Defensive: When you receive feedback it can often be challenging to not get defensive. You may get defensive and be unable to hear feedback because of whom the feedback is coming from or how it's being delivered. If you can separate the feedback from the messenger, separate *what the message is* from *how the message is being sent;* you may find that there is valuable information to use if you are open to it. Once you allow yourself to hear it, then you can take it or leave it. *Listening* to someone's feedback is different than agreeing with it, responding to it, and acting on it. If you receive a piece of feedback you don't agree with, you don't have to do anything about it. Know that some of the feedback will apply to you and some of it won't. Ask for clarification instead of giving your opinion. When receiving feedback you don't have to defend yourself or have an explanation. But you also don't have to automatically dismiss it either. Sometimes feeling defensive is a sign that the messenger has hit on something that rings true.

Disinterested: You aren't always looking for feedback or don't always want feedback. Instead of feedback getting distorted through your filters or getting defensive and not being able to hear it, this has to do with the fact that you don't want it in the first place. You are either happy with the status quo and aren't interested in receiving feedback because you aren't really interested in improving your performance, or you feel that just listening to the feedback is like an admission that you are doing something wrong. Allowing others to see that you are vulnerable to mistakes is anxiety provoking and as humans we are designed to alleviate those feelings of anxiety. You either act on the feedback to prevent those feelings in the future, or hide from it so you don't have to feel anxious at all. Being disinterested in feedback means that you feel compelled to justify your actions or deny there is any feedback to be received in order to alleviate your anxiety. Acknowledging you have areas to work on is not an admission of failure; it is an admission that you have more potential.

Asking for Feedback

If you participate in your sport long enough, somewhere along the way someone will give you some friendly pointers to try and help you out. When you play a team sport, it's the job of the coaching staff to give you feedback to help you improve your individual performance so you are able to contribute to the team's goals. There will also be people that will give you unsolicited feedback more to boost their own ego than to help your performance. Feedback is inextricably linked to sport; it's a package deal. If you really want to improve and start taking control of your performance, be proactive about asking for feedback.

When you ask for feedback and do it from a place of wanting to improve, it can be easier to take in someone else's feedback. You put the power into your hands when you choose to be open to feedback and choose to not let someone else's feedback define you. You can gain amazing insights from people when you ask them for their honest opinion about your performance. You can actively seek out feedback from friends, coaches, and teammates, but the best candidates are people whose opinions you value and trust, who care about your goals, and will be honest with what they say. If hearing it stings a little, it's because how you perform in your sport is something that's important to you. The bonus is that when you are proactive about getting feedback — you may actually be more open to receiving it. That outside perspective is invaluable and sometimes that's what it takes to have a breakthrough in your performance — to be able to see things through someone else's eyes, when you are ready to see it yourself.

In order to get informative and valuable feedback, it helps to give the person you are asking some structure. What kind of feedback do you want? Do you need feedback about a specific skill? Feedback on your overall performance? Don't ask for feedback unless you are ready to hear it. You need to genuinely want to hear what they have to say — both the good and the bad. If your motive in asking for feedback is so people will tell you what you want to hear — you aren't ready. Before asking someone for feedback, you need to do some solo evaluating and reflecting first. When you're ready for feedback, don't just ask the usual suspects. Think outside the box, who else might have some insight into you and your performance? Here is an example of a structured format you can use to be able to seek out feedback:

Feedback Questionnaire
Feedback isn't just for skill improvement. Feedback is also good for getting a look at the big picture. Create your own feedback questionnaire by typing out the following questions:

- What are my top three strengths?
- In what ways do I hold myself back?
- What are three things I need to improve?
- What is the most important thing for me to work on now?

First, fill out the questionnaire for yourself. Actually write out your answers and then figure out who else you would like to have answer these questions. You can get feedback from your coaches, teammates — anyone you feel will answer honestly. Give them the questionnaire and ask them to write their answers down so you can really sit with it and have time to process all of the feedback. It can be overwhelming to get a lot of feedback at once, so start with one person and once you have sat with his or her feedback, then add people from there. After taking time to evaluate all of the answers you receive, you can then set goals related to the feedback. A few years back I was working with an athlete that wanted to work on his leadership skills. Many of his teammates looked to him as a leader and he sometimes felt he wasn't equipped for the job. I had him create a similar version of the feedback questionnaire to fill out and then he had to select one of his coaches to ask if he would fill it out as well. After getting feedback from his coach, he learned that he was doing a better job than he thought and also received some information from his coach on concrete areas we could work on to improve his leadership skills.

It's not always easy to ask for and hear honest feedback, so when you do it, give yourself a pat on the back. Additionally, it's also not always easy to dole out honest feedback so you should give the person you asked a pat on the back as well. Make sure you show your gratitude for the time and effort it took for them to write out honest and thoughtful answers. Take the time to thank anyone that followed through with your request because they just helped you to be a better athlete.

Creating Your Story

There is another significant source of feedback that guides your future performances. After every competition, you create a story about that experience. The story you choose to tell can end up being a theme that gets woven through to your next competition and even through your whole season. That story influences your expectations for the future. This idea is important because *the story you tell isn't always accurate*. Reflecting on your performances can help you to successively build upon them to shape and create successful performances moving forward. However, reflecting upon your performances can also contribute to increased feelings of anxiety and fear and have you headed in a downward spiral. All of it depends on which story you choose to tell. There are a few different factors that will influence this storyline and one important factor is how your brain actually stores memories.

Memories are retrieved through pathways in the brain. If your brain is reaching out to remember something and it's not quite grasping it, your brain will go to other networks of pathways to try and retrieve it. However, some long-term memories come immediately sprinting down the pathway. The stronger the emotional impact of the situation, the more likely it is to get deeply imprinted in your memory; this is why we can recall specific details and remember things like where you were, whom you were with, and what you were thinking during certain events. For me, the day my sister was brought home from the hospital, the 1989 Loma Prieta Earthquake, the day I almost got hit by a car, the day I got married, these are memories that stand out because there were strong emotions tied to each experience.

When you recall some of your own strongest memories, you will notice that you had strong emotions present as well. In the first chapter, when you are asked to recall your best and worst performances, these events stick out in your mind because of the strong emotional reaction you had when they occurred. There are hundreds of other performances that don't particularly stand out because there are no strong emotions tied to them. Maintaining the status quo doesn't have as big of an impact. Additionally, if you had a fantastic performance all the way up until the end, that emotion you feel at the end gets extrapolated to explain how you feel about the entire experience. When you think back on that competition, all you remember is that it was awful and you don't even want to think about it. The emotion you feel as a result of the circumstances at the end of the game becomes the story. It's the end of the experience that creates the memory.

Expectations of future events are based on past experience. Unless you have a deliberate plan in place to reflect on your performances to tell an accurate account of the story, you are relying on your memory to tell the story. Many moments make up the experience, but most of them are forgotten. Like any good story, the moments that are remembered are the ones that are significant — the suspense, the action, the plot changes, and the ending. If you are in a slump or have been experiencing performance anxiety, the memories of your mistakes and failures are stronger and more likely to come sprinting down the pathway. Those memories inevitably become part of the story you create about your experience and that story will influence your level of motivation and confidence going into your next event.

Your Perceptions of Success and Failure

The way your brain stores memories is just one factor that can impact the story you create. Your story also includes your interpretation of what caused you to fail or succeed in the goals (*and secret goals*) you set for yourself that day. Your *perceptions* of the causes that led you to succeed or fail are an integral part of the equation that creates your expectations of success or failure in the future. There are two essential elements within that part of the equation: The first is whether or not you believe that the cause is a factor that is capable of being changed. The second is whether or not you believe that the cause is a factor that is under your direct control.

Athletes who attribute bad performances to things that are temporary and within their control to change are more likely to feel positive and motivated going into their next performance. Knowing that a poor performance is due to something that you can work on and improve (e.g.

changing tactical decisions, improving a specific skill) or is due to some-thing that isn't guaranteed to occur next time (e.g. bad call by a referee, poor weather conditions) are attributions allowing you to recognize that one bad performance doesn't mean every performance will be bad. On the other side, athletes that attribute a bad performance to something that is outside of their control and unlikely to change (e.g. issues with the coaching staff, feeling you're untalented and will never be good enough) are more likely to be unmotivated and insecure going into their next performance. These negative attributions get carried forward into future expectations of failure.

When you feel as though the situation is permanent and you have no control over influencing or correcting the issue, it can be incredibly poisonous to your motivation. These types of attributions can lead to learned helplessness, the belief that no matter what you do, nothing will change so why even bother trying. Athletes that attribute a good per-formance to things that are unlikely to change and are in their control are more likely to expect future success. Your immediate attributions after an event — your perception of what you believe is the cause of your success or failure — strongly influences your emotional reaction. Experiences tied to strong emotions are more likely to be the ones we remember. Humans are designed to encode emotional events into mem-ory because it is more likely that those events are essential for survival. If you are under stress during the experience, it can affect your memory. When you think back you will remember the emotion, but not what happened. You'll then base your attributions more on the emotion than the actual occurrence.

Your attributions not only influence your expectations of future suc-cess or failure, they also influence how much effort you put forth. They influence how motivated you are to continue working on your skills and participating in your sport. They influence how confident you feel in your ability to change and improve. Being conscious of what you attribute your successes and failures to is essential for putting yourself in the best position to be successful in the future. Occasionally athletes will ask me if changing his or her attributions is just a way to make excuses for a bad performance. Here's a typical scenario; I'm working with a cyclist and we go through and evaluate a performance that he feels went badly. Throughout our post-competition debrief we discover that he didn't get as much sleep as he usually does the night before a race and that the tire pressure may not have been ideal for the conditions. He agrees with the evaluation, but wants to know, at what point is he making excuses for a "poor" performance? Changing your perception of the factors that caused your bad performance doesn't mean you are throwing away all responsibility. If anything, it makes it more likely that you will be motivated and confident enough to make the necessary changes in order to improve future performances.

Looking Back and Moving Forward

When people think about getting feedback, they usually assume that the feedback is coming from someone else, such as a coach, assistant coach, teammate, family member, friend, etc. However, there is another incredibly valuable source for feedback that's often underutilized and overlooked — and that is *you*. Your performance doesn't just improve with time. You can take two athletes from the same sport with identical athletic potential, have them compete for ten years, and then see one of them excel while the other stagnates. The number of years under your belt is not the only factor that accounts for your expertise as an athlete. Equally, if not more important, is the *quality* of the time involved. The rate of your improvement is also influenced by whether or not you are consciously reflecting on your performances and implementing the knowledge you gained through deliberate, goal-directed practice.

When reflecting on your performance, are you reflecting on the experience, or on the memory of the experience? As you learned, your memory alone cannot be relied upon to accurately reflect the actual experience. Going through the simple process of reflecting on each performance gives you a more accurate account of the event. It enables you to reconstruct your perceptions and attitudes of the event that reflect the true story and the story that will positively impact your confidence and performance moving forward.

Reflection needs to occur after *every* performance. Some athletes may be inclined to only reflect after their good performances or bad performances. Or they may skip filling out their post-performance evaluations if they feel like nothing eventful happened. However, *every* performance has valuable lessons to be learned. Ideally you should fill out your post-performance evaluations within a few days after your performance. Fill it out close enough that you'll remember the details, but far enough away that you can gain some perspective. Reflecting immediately after your performance may result in a different evaluation versus reflecting a few days or a week later. Immediately after your performance, your evaluation will be influenced by the feelings and emotions associated with the events that occurred during that particular performance. Filling out your post-performance evaluations consistently will eventually help influence your immediate performance attributions as well.

Athletes often neglect taking the time to reflect on a performance. When you move from one competition to the next without getting any feedback, it's as if you're just riding on the merry-go-round, hoping that at some point your wooden carousel horse will jump the track to find a better landscape. Think about what information would be valuable for you to have. What trends would you like to be able to have some insight into? You can create your own evaluations or just add on a reflective piece to your current performance log. You can make it as detailed or as simple as you like. When you are consistent with filling out your performance evaluations, you are collecting invaluable data that you can use to study your own performance. After every game or race, at a *minimum*, you should be asking yourself:

- What did I do well?
- What would I have done differently?
- What did I learn that I want to carry forward?

Without deliberate reflection, we tend to judge our performance solely based on how we did compared to others. Reflecting after each performance helps you to make sure you are gauging your success on the goals you set for yourself. It also helps you to build your awareness around the factors that can positively or negatively influence your performance.

Giving Credit Where Credit is Due

Part of reflecting on your performances needs to include time to recognize and appreciate your accomplishments. This recognition is much more than rewarding the outcome of your performance. It's about owning your accomplishments and being proud of what you have done, including the effort you put forth along the way: Your hard work, resilience, and perseverance. Your discipline, sacrifice, and dedication to your sport. The focus and drive it took to work towards your goals as well as achieve the performance outcomes that you wanted. I see many athletes take *full* ownership over their mistakes and failures, and take *no* ownership over their accomplishments and successes. They either dismiss them, aren't conscious of them at all, or they feel like an admission of accomplishment means they are denying that there is still work to be done. When you constantly want to see yourself improve, it can be challenging to recognize when you've actually improved. There is always work to be done. There is always room for learning, growth, and improvement, which makes it even more important to recognize the milestones along the way, and to recognize both arriving at the destination and the journey it took to get there.

When you've reached a milestone — it could be accomplishing a specific goal, getting through a certain event, or reaching the end of your season — think about how you want to recognize and celebrate your hard work. Pretend that you are the president of your own fan club and it's your job to make sure that you are sufficiently celebrated. Here are some ideas to pay yourself tribute:

Tell your story: Take the time to acknowledge the events by telling your story. This could mean telling the story of one particular game or telling the story of your season. Here are some examples of ways you can tell your story:

- Tell a friend: Sometimes telling your story might involve just one close friend. A person that intimately knows the sacrifices you made and challenges you faced along your journey, someone that will be just as excited for your accomplishments as you are.

- Blog: Many athletes have blogs so their family, friends, and fans can get the latest news. You can start your own blog and post your own race report or game day synopsis to share your story.

- Journal: The act of writing your story helps validate it and even helps with the storage of that memory. It gives you a record of how you felt when it actually happened that you could look back over and connect with.

Tangible rewards: You can also acknowledge your efforts with tangible rewards. When using tangible rewards, be sure to reward yourself for your effort and hard work and not just for a specific outcome. Using a tangible reward to recognize your accomplishments is different than using it to reward or punish your performance. It's a subtle, but important distinction. Your intention behind the reward and your choice of reward is what can make that distinction. Keeping this in mind, make a list of your own potential rewards. Here are some ideas to get your started:

- Equipment upgrade: Having new gear can be motivating in and of itself. New ski gloves, new components for your bike, or even new workout clothes can be a great reward for a season of dedicated work.

- Go to sports camp: Treat yourself to your own training camp. Not only can you meet great people in your sport, but you can get some world-class instruction as well.

- Get a coach: Give yourself the reward of a physical or mental coach and not only will you get a great reward, but you can get the knowledge and support to improve your performance and help you achieve your goals as well.

- Indulge: Get yourself a massage once a week for a month. Buy yourself something that will make your travel more enjoyable like noise-cancelling headphones. Reward yourself with something that will benefit you as well as feel indulgent.

Symbolic act: In the last chapter you read about the power of symbolic rituals. An additional way to acknowledge your accomplishments is to choose a symbolic act, some sort of ritual or gesture that is done in the conscious act of acknowledging your accomplishments. Here are some examples from athletes I have worked with:

- Go out to your favorite restaurant with family and friends
- Reflect on your athletic journey as you hike to the top of a mountain
- Have a traditional post-event or post-season burger and a beer
- Throw yourself a party to celebrate
- Take a fun weekend trip or vacation

Whatever you choose to do, it should be personally meaningful to you and purposefully done in the service of acknowledging your accomplishments. Rewards that are only used for a specific outcome can potentially be perceived as controlling, which will be detrimental to your intrinsic motivation. Be sure to reward ALL of your efforts. Don't just reward the outcome — reward the entire journey. For every time you wanted to stop moving and you went a little longer. For every time you wanted to stay home and you got your workout in anyway. For every time you wanted to be negative and you turned it around. For every time you kept working on something holding faith that you would see the fruits of your labor. For every time you skipped a workout (even though you were terribly distraught and conflicted) because you knew it was the right decision. ALL of your efforts deserve recognition, so be sure to recognize them.

Intentionally Improving Your Performance

When you aren't proactive about seeking out feedback and reflecting on your performances, it's like making and baking a cake without writing down the recipe. Each time you bake the cake you are starting over instead of refining and polishing the process. The feedback during your training and competition will always be there, but whether or not you are capable of receiving it and willing to act on it is an entirely different story. When you take the time to reflect on your competition, you provide yourself with feedback that can be used to improve performance. Without this feedback you're destined to continue to make the same mistakes and eventually plateau in your performance. Taking the time to reflect on your performances and actively seeking out feedback will help speed up the process of learning, adapting, and improving on past performances.

You can't improve your performance without knowing how you are doing relative to where you want to be. Receiving feedback is how we learn. It's a skill that needs to be honed if you want to be deliberate about improving in your sport. Working on the often-neglected skills discussed in this chapter can contribute to preventing your feelings of performance anxiety. Reflection can help you come to terms with a bad performance and help you repeat a good one. Neglecting to obtain feedback and write reflections are huge omissions in your mental game. It takes time and effort, but it's well worth it. Changing your perception of what it means to get feedback, learning how to be open to feedback, understanding your role in creating your story, these can all influence how positive and optimistic you feel about your ability and your performance.

Chapter 8: Take-Aways

- Feedback is information about the progress of your performance. All learning and improvement comes from your ability to receive and act on that feedback.

- Feedback is not a bad word. Acknowledging that you have areas to improve is recognizing that you have more potential.

- Being proactive about seeking out feedback can make it easier to hear. Open yourself up to hearing feedback by untangling what the feedback is from how you feel about it.

- The story you create about your performances and who you are as an athlete influences your motivation, confidence, and future expectations moving forward. Be deliberate about creating your story.

- You need to be your own biggest fan. Be proud of your accomplishments. Take the time to recognize the milestones along your journey.

Chapter 8: Tools

Tool: Post-Competition Evaluation

In order to get an accurate account of your performance during a competition and be able to build on your performances, you need to evaluate your competitive performance. Being deliberate about reflecting on your performances will help you to practice creating beneficial attributions and telling the version of the story that contributes to confidence instead of anxiety. Taking the time to evaluate both what you did well and what you need to work on will help you to maintain your confidence and take responsibility for improving your performance.

Step 1: To create a system for consistently reflecting on your performances, first choose a cut-off time – a set time when you need to have filled out your reflection after your performance. Adjust when necessary, but stick to this time as much as possible.

Step 2: The next step is to choose the medium. Are you going to add a reflective piece to your already existing training log? Do you want to have written reflections in a binder or folder? Electronic reflections to fill out on your computer or mobile device? Choose a method that is appealing and sustainable for you.

Step 3: Using your chosen method, after each performance answer the following:

- What were your goals for this event?
- How successful were you in achieving your goals?
- What did you do well?
- What was the biggest challenge?
- Is there anything that you would have done differently?
- What did you learn that you want to carry forward?

Step 4: You can now use your reflections to guide you in creating goals to work on in practice. You can also incorporate them into your PPP (Pre-Performance Plan) by including a time to read through part or all of your reflections to help you prepare for your next performance.

Tool: Mid-Season and Post-Season Evaluations
If you want to continue to both understand and improve your performance you need to take the time to do a global mid-season and post-season assessment. These assessments will help you take a look at the big picture and pull together the overall themes you see in your Post-Competition Evaluations.

Step 1: Pick a date when you will do a mid-season evaluation and write that date in your training calendar.

Step 2: On that day, read through your Post-Competition Evaluations up to that date.

Step 3: Fill out your Mid-Season Evaluation by answering the following:

- What are your goals for this season?
- What kind of progress have you made towards your goals?
- What are the strengths of your physical performance?
- What are the strengths of your mental game?
- What has been the most challenging part of the season so far?
- What areas do you want to change/improve?
- How will you work towards these changes?
- Other Comments:

Step 4: Pick a date when you will fill out your Post-Season Evaluation and write that date in your training calendar.

Step 5: On that day, read over your Mid-Season Evaluations and then read through your Post-Competition Evaluations up to that date.

Step 6: Fill out your Post-Season Evaluation by answering the following:

- What are some of your accomplishments from this season?
- What were your biggest challenges?
- What has been your greatest area of improvement?
- Which mental skills techniques worked for you and why?
- What part of your mental game would you like to strengthen?
- What would you like to see continue into next season?
- What would you like to see change for next season?

- What do you look forward to accomplishing next season?
- What do you want to work on in the off-season?
- Other comments:

Step 7: Use your Post-Season Evaluation to create your goal plan heading into your next season.

chapter 9

FROM OBSTACLES TO OPPORTUNITIES

"All of us get knocked down, but it's resiliency that really matters."
—Roger Staubach, former NFL quarterback

Natalie du Toit has dreamed of going to the Olympics since she was six years old. She set multiple records as a young swimmer and competed in her first international race at the age of 14. Her career was pointing in the exact direction of her Olympic dream and at 16 she came close when she almost qualified for three events leading up to the 2000 Sydney Olympics. She was one of the most promising athletes in South Africa; it was just a matter of time before she realized her dream.

In February of 2001, Natalie had a morning that started like any other morning. She had just finished her workout and was driving away on her scooter heading to school. As she rode down the street from the pool, Natalie was struck by a car and in that one moment, her life was changed forever. The accident was devastating and resulted in the amputation of her left leg, just above the knee. When you hear her talk about her experience, you are immediately struck by her perseverance, determination, and resilience; "I have always had a dream to take part in an Olympic Games, and losing my leg didn't change anything." For many of us, upon hearing Natalie's story our immediate thoughts go to a lost dream, but not so for Natalie — her determination was unstoppable. As soon as her surgery was complete, all she could think about was getting back in the pool. Just three years after her accident she made it to Athens and won five gold medals in the 2004 Paralympic Games.

Natalie's journey didn't stop there. In 2008, she became one of the most inspiring stories of the summer. Natalie stunned the world and made history by qualifying for both the Olympics and Paralympics that year. During the 2008 Beijing Olympics, with tears in her eyes, Natalie carried the flag for South Africa during the opening ceremonies. She went on to finish 16th in the 10K open water swim with a time of two hours and 49.9 seconds. She also added another five gold medals from the 2008 Paralympics to match her 2004 Paralympics accomplishment. During the 2012 Paralympic Games in London she went home with three gold medals and just missed out on getting a fourth gold medal during the final race of her career. Natalie never set out to be an inspirational athlete. She wasn't out to prove anything; she just kept moving towards her personal goals and wouldn't stop no matter what life tried to throw her way; "Even when bad things happen you have to try use those bad things in a positive manner and really just take the positive out of it."

Why does one athlete crumble under pressure while another one rises to the challenge? What makes one athlete feel called to action after facing a setback, while another one feels the urge to call it quits? Natalie's story is just one among hundreds of inspirational stories about athletes that have encountered and overcome adversity. When you choose to compete you are choosing to put yourself to the test and see what you are capable of. This road does not come without obstacles. As an athlete, you will inevitably encounter some challenges along the way. If competition weren't challenging, it wouldn't mean as much to achieve a personal record or win a championship game. One of the greatest things you can do for yourself as an athlete is to embrace the entire journey. Embrace the obstacles, challenges, and setbacks. Embrace the errors and losses. Embrace the whole package – the good and the bad — and know that nothing feels better than the moment you rise above whatever obstacles are put in your way. Setbacks are an inevitable aspect of sport. However, an athlete's ability to deal with setbacks is often what distinguishes him from his competitors.

Seeing the Opportunity

For some people, setbacks are viewed in terms of "what-ifs". *What-ifs* tend to elicit your stress response because when you think of them, you're usually concerned with whether or not you will be able to handle them. Assessing that you might not be able to handle the stressor in front of you is what leads you to start feeling anxious. One of the most important things to know about encountering obstacles is that *how you think about setbacks affects how you react to them*. There are minor setbacks and major setbacks, but sometimes you turn a minor one into a major one because of your perception of it and your reaction to it. When faced with a setback, there is a continuum of perception and where you fall on the continuum depicts how you will react to that setback. The continuum is established by the language you use when thinking about the obstacle in front of you. The language you choose to define the situation impacts how you feel, how you think, and how you react to that situation. Here are the ways in which you can define an obstacle:

It's going to **suck**.

"This is going to suck and I don't want to do this." When you decide the obstacle is going to *suck*, every fiber of your being does not want to face what is in front of you. You're fighting against the situation and that creates psychological and physiological tension making the entire situation even worse.

It's going to be **hard**.

"This is going to be hard and I'm really not looking forward to it." When you define the obstacle as *hard*, you're still fighting against the situation, but you reluctantly move forward. You move forward, but you're miserable about it.

It's going to be a **challenge**.

"This is going to be challenging, but I can do this." When you define the obstacle as a *challenge*, you know it will be hard, but you are ready to face it. Your reaction to the difficulty of it is to rise to the challenge.

It's going to be an **opportunity**.

"This is going to be a great opportunity." When you can see the *opportunity* in the obstacle, not only are you ready for the challenge, but you also embrace it. You seek out ways to use the obstacle to improve.

To test this theory of how the thoughts and language you choose influences how you feel and approach a situation, try out this exercise: Grab a piece of paper so you can write down your thoughts. Think about a potential obstacle or setback you are currently facing or might be facing in the future. Just choose the first thing that comes to mind. As you hold that scenario in your mind, read each of the sentences below in reference to your situation. For each sentence, write down the thoughts that come to you as you define your situation with that sentence.

- It's going to **suck.**
- It's going to be **hard.**
- It's going to be a **challenge.**
- It's going to be an **opportunity.**

Once you write out the thoughts that come to you with each sentence, go back and read through your answers. As you read through, jot down what emotions you feel as you read each section. If you really tried this exercise, you may have noticed that your thoughts and feelings about your situation changed depending on which sentence you were choosing to define it with. There is your continuum — from worst-case scenario to best-case scenario. When you first start working on this, you might start on one end of the continuum and have to gradually work your way up like you did in this exercise. With practice, you will start that process further and further along the continuum until it becomes quicker for you to adjust and see the opportunity rather than the difficulty. In the next paragraph you'll read through a specific situation to give you an example of what that process looks like.

For this example, let's say you are a cyclist and you know there is going to be a big hill you have to climb in the middle of your race and climbing isn't your strength. If your chosen perception of the situation is that, "This is going to *suck*", you will be dreading the climb miles before it even comes. As soon as you hit the climb you've already created extra muscular tension in your body and you are so focused on how much it sucks that you feel every excruciating pedal stroke as you watch the other cyclists pass you by. If you're in that same race and your chosen perception is that the climb is going to be *hard*, you're still not looking forward to it, but you're not obsessing about it for miles either. It continues to be your least favorite part of cycling, but you'll force yourself to do it because you have to. As you move through the continuum, when faced with that same obstacle in that same race, things start to subtly shift when you decide, "This climb is going to be a *challenge*." You know the climb will be difficult, but you're ready. You know what your game plan is and you know you can execute it. You're able to stay within yourself and not worry about how anyone else is climbing. When you get to the point where you can think about that climb as an *opportunity*, you're not only ready for the challenge, but you're looking forward to it. Not only do you know your game plan and know you can execute it, you also seek out ways to learn from it and improve your performance. You know that this climb is preparing you for the next one.

In every scenario, the situation is exactly the same: you're a cyclist with a climb in your race and climbing isn't your strength. In the moment, you might not have any control over the situation, but you do have control over your reaction to it and that reaction can change the entire scene. If you go back and look over your own continuum, you can see that with each perception comes an entirely different story. In the last chapter you learned how the stories you create affect your motivation and confidence moving forward. Which story is more likely to have a positive impact on your performance? Which story do you want to carry forward? The athlete or team that comes out on top is often the one that encounters the obstacle, sees the opportunity, and makes the adjustment.

As you know from what you have read in this book so far, there are many different factors that go into how you feel when you encounter a setback. For example, you know that:

- Whether or not you feel capable of meeting the challenge will influence your thoughts and that some of those negative thoughts then become automatic.
- Your thoughts can trigger a physiological response in your body and lead you to feel anxious.
- Having a clear goal in your mind will strengthen your commitment to overcoming setbacks.

The continuum exercise helps you to recognize how your thoughts can define an entire situation and impact how you feel and what you do in that situation. It also helps you see that there are other ways to perceive it and that you have more control over that perception than you think.

Encountering Setbacks

A cyclist working his or her way up the continuum for climbing is one thing, but what about other types of obstacles and setbacks? If you participate in sports long enough, you will eventually face one or more of the setbacks you will read about in the following paragraphs. They encompass some of the main categories of setbacks that athletes will face at some point during their participation in sports:

Under-Performing

Under-performing is characterized by a difference in the expectation of how you wanted to perform and how you actually performed. There are many different potential causes of under-performing and you want to diagnose the cause so you can figure out the cure. Sometimes the cause is in your control — you're over or under trained, you played down to your opponent; and sometimes the cause is out of your control — your team experienced a lot of injuries, you had a string of bad luck, you had some other emergencies or life stressors that impacted your ability to train and compete, etc. Whatever the cause, when you don't perform as well as you hoped it could feel like a significant setback. You're probably frustrated and/or angry that you didn't perform the way that you envisioned. You may even find yourself questioning your participation in your sport and wondering if things will ever improve. Having a poor performance at a particular event or experiencing an entire season of under-performance can be disappointing and devastating. However, when you experience under-performance there is a tremendous opportunity to gain invaluable feedback about what worked and what didn't so you can start working on your comeback.

If you are under-performing, you need to assess whether something in your physical training, mental training, or preparation actually needs to change or whether you are being unrealistic with your expectations of progress. To start that assessment, fill out your post-competition or post-season evaluation and ask other people for feedback. Think about what worked and what didn't so you can learn and adjust. However, if you find that you are on the right track and were being unrealistic with your expectations, you need to be patient and redefine what it means to be successful. If you find that you get frustrated when your performance stops improving by leaps and bounds, you need to step back and remind yourself that significant improvement comes from many small actions taken and built upon over time. You have to stop beating yourself up and accept that things didn't go the way you wanted them to so you can then see the opportunities for improvement moving forward.

Mistakes

When I was in high school I took a drama class as one of my electives. One of the exercises we had to do in class was to get up on stage in small groups and improvise acting out a scene. A group usually started with a topic suggested by the rest of the class or the group was assigned a random prop and then they had to jump into action and make up the scene. There are many different skills you learn and develop through having to improvise in this way, one of them being: *there are no mistakes*. With improv, whether it's in music or in theater, when there is a "mistake" you either keep going without missing a beat or you adapt and adopt it into the performance.

Making an error or mistake during a clutch situation during competition can feel heart breaking. Many athletes and coaches profess that it's OK to make mistakes, but not many of them live that virtue and *really* believe it. How you feel about it often depends on the consequences of the mistake and whether or not you feel like it impacted the outcome of the game. The following are some common reactions athletes have after making a mistake. You may:

- Feel embarrassed and hope nothing else comes your way
- Be angry with yourself for making such a stupid mistake and then try to force a way to make up for it
- See the looks on the faces around you and feel upset that you've let people down
- Feel like your mistake is the obstacle that will prevent you from accomplishing your goal

I've seen games lost from the singular fact that an athlete or team was unable to recover from an error. When mistakes are made in competition, it only disrupts the momentum if you let it. Like improv, a mistake is only a setback if you decide it is. If you decide that it isn't, then a mistake is just an opportunity to figure out another way to get it done.

Slumps

Slumps can feel devastating and insurmountable. Sometimes it starts with a mistake or an "off" day and that one instance turns into two, and two into three, etc. It's your negative thoughts, judgments, and fears that impact your feelings of anxiety and fuels the momentum in a negative direction. As you know, the repercussions of that anxiety are increased distractibility, increased muscular tension, and decreased confidence. When you're in a slump, your fear of failure can manifest into an expectation of failure, which then speeds up the momentum of the downward spiral.

When you're experiencing a slump, your initial instinct might be to try harder and force your way out of it. When you see that not only does that not work, but makes things worse — you eventually give in and give up. You become focused on the impact of the slump and how it affects the outcome of your performance. Your thoughts are time traveling into the future consumed with the fear that you're going to make the same mistake or lose another game. When you're time traveling, you are incapable of staying in the moment and allowing yourself to feel the feedback you're getting from your body.

You need to stop trying to fight against the fact you're in a slump and know that it will pass. Instead of trying to force your way out of it, accept it as something that every athlete will experience at some point and right now that athlete is you. Once you accept it, you can relax your shoulders a little bit and become an observer of your performance. You can't see your way out of it until you accept that it's happening and trust that you'll eventually come out on the other side. The acceptance doesn't mean that you're happy about it. It means that you can relax a little about where you're at and stop putting pressure on yourself, which will allow you to open up and receive feedback and focus on what is in your control.

Lose Your Starting Position

For some athletes it can feel demoralizing to lose their starting position on a team. There are different factors that can result in an athlete losing their starting position, but it usually boils down to a decision made by the coach; a decision that in the coach's mind is a decision made in the best interest of the team. Someone else on the team is more skilled than you in your position at this moment. It may be that someone came up through the ranks and outperformed you, you got comfortable in your role and got complacent, or you had to take some time off to nurse an injury, and someone else surpassed you. In any case, the result is that you lost your spot.

Depending on how you're feeling about your own performance at that moment, you may feel that losing your spot was justified or unjustified. If you feel like you've been working hard and someone came up through the ranks and surpassed you, you can experience many different emotions. You might feel like you'll never be good enough and that it's the beginning of the end. You might even feel relief that it finally happened. If you got complacent and someone passed you by, it may have come as a shock to lose your starting position. You may be angry with your coach and feel like it was an unfair decision. You might feel embarrassed that you lost your spot or even be angry with your teammate and feel like your spot was taken from you. Eventually you may even be angry with yourself for slacking off and not seeing it coming. Regardless of all this, the decision has been made and it is out of your control. What's in your control is accepting that it actually might be the best decision for the team at this time. If you play a team sport you know that sometimes the individual makes a sacrifice for the goals of the team. What's also in your control is your outlook and deciding that it's temporary and talking to your coach about how to win your spot back. Now you have an opportunity to improve your skills and win it back.

Burnout

In Chapter Two you read all about the ebb and flow of your motivation and how your motivation will fluctuate throughout one season, let alone throughout your entire athletic career. Some of the motivational dips you encounter are minor setbacks that are quickly and easily overcome. When you start to feel like going to practice is a chore and you'd rather stay home, you may be experiencing some burnout. Here are some potential factors that can lead you there:

- Physical exhaustion
- Feeling overwhelmed
- No support system
- Issues with teammates
- Issues with coaches
- Long season
- Feeling bored
- Not seeing improvement
- High pressure
- High life stress

It's possible to have multiple factors causing your feelings of burnout. Regardless of the cause, your motivation is low and you aren't having any fun. It's important to know what the cause is of your motivational low so you can start to figure out what to do about it. If your burnout is due to physical exhaustion, your interventions will be different than if your burnout is due to being bored or not seeing improvements in your performance. When you're feeling some burnout, you can start to figure out the cause by looking at the previous list and see which factors you identify with to try and diagnose why you're no longer having any fun. Experiencing burnout is an opportunity to learn how you operate and be proactive about preventing burnout in the future.

Injury

A longer-term setback you may experience at some point in your athletic career is sustaining an injury. No one likes to think about it, but injury is a part of the risk that comes with being an athlete. When you sustain an injury, there is a whole roller coaster of emotions you will experience from the onset of the injury through your return to competition. The thought of not being able to compete and feeling that every passing second equals you losing ground on your competition with your training and fitness can be overwhelming. Obviously, no one wants to get injured and it is a great challenge to see the opportunity that lies within being injured. However, I've had many athletes make amazing comebacks after sustaining an injury. They used the time they had to take to recover and strengthened something else that wasn't affected by their injuries; they worked on their core strength, they studied film, they refined a technique, they worked on their mental game, etc. These athletes sought out opportunities to improve in other ways while they were injured and were smart about their transition back into their sports and came back stronger because of it.

Injuries are unique in that you can have setbacks to the setback. Once you're injured, it feels like a setback to your season or career. Additionally, as you're rehabilitating from your injury you can have setbacks during your recovery as well. Just like any other setback, the most important thing you can do is adjust your goal and focus on what's in your control. Your job was to perform in your sport and now your job is to recover from your injury and to do it to the best of your ability. Just because your body is out of the game doesn't mean you have to take your head out too. Think about other parts of your performance that you can work on while you are recovering and transitioning back into your sport. Looking for the opportunities helps to shift the control back into your hands.

Overtraining & Illness

As an athlete, there are times when you are pushing your body to the limit. Unfortunately, some athletes and coaches don't listen to their bodies and keep pushing when they need to back off. You probably know from experience that when you don't listen to your body, your body will make you listen. The terms *burnout* and *overtraining* are sometimes used interchangeably although each one is its own unique and challenging setback. With overtraining, athletes often *want* to train and compete; they are extremely motivated, but their bodies have shut down.

When you have pushed your body beyond its capacity and haven't balanced out your training with recovery, overtraining can lead to Overtraining Syndrome (OTS). OTS is the outcome of overtraining and is defined by a decrease in physical performance as a result of over-training and under-recovery. OTS is especially frustrating because the process of recovery is different for every athlete and can take anywhere from weeks to months. Overtraining can also lead to other setbacks such as injury and illness.

If you're recovering from overtraining or a long-term illness, the road back to competition can be long and challenging. You are motivated and ready to get back in the game and it's frustrating to wait for your body to catch up. With any setback, it's important to be able to step back and look at the big picture. You need to remind yourself that this journey won't take forever, but that *it will take longer* if you push too hard too soon. Patience and trust are key during this process. Similar to coming back from an injury, focus on your progress and improvement. Celebrate hitting those milestones instead of getting hooked by the monster and thinking about where you should be or how far you have to go.

Dealing with Setbacks

Each of these scenarios can leave you feeling either like a victim or a warrior. These setbacks will happen to every athlete so when it happens to you, it is just your time. If you find yourself feeling like a victim of your setbacks, you need to challenge your beliefs. You need to remind yourself that these things aren't happening to you, they are just happening. When encountering obstacles, resilient and mentally tough athletes are able to stay focused and keep moving forward. They are able to accept the fact that there is an obstacle and then look for the opportunity. Looking for opportunities is not just about being an eternal optimist; it's about regaining control by being resilient.

When these setbacks occur, you might feel the pull to over-personalize them by thinking, "Why is this happening to me?" The world is not against you; the world is simply in motion. When you encounter a setback, you may experience feelings of frustration, confusion, disappointment, and fear — resilient athletes will regroup and accept the situation and then think "What now ... what's my next move?"

Thinking About Plan B

Athletes operate from fear when they feel they are not equipped to handle the obstacles they face. Getting sick, getting injured, losing your starting position, making a mental error during a crucial game; these are all potential challenges you will face and how you deal with those challenges defines your level of mental toughness and resilience. For some people, just thinking about the potential obstacles they may encounter will induce anxiety. Since your body is designed to alleviate that feeling of anxiety, sometimes your response to that feeling is to not think about those situations. When you are performing in the moment, this can be an effective tactic to use. Stopping that line of thinking can help you shift your focus to where it needs to be in that moment. However, sometimes you find that when you don't want to think about something, that is exactly what you need to be thinking about. Since you are designed to alleviate anxiety through your fight-or-flight response, you can also choose to fight. When thinking about a potential setback, "fighting," means planning. Consciously creating your Plan B for potential setbacks means you will be ready for the obstacle when it comes. When you create a Plan B, you are addressing if/then scenarios; if "X" happens, then I will do "Y". If you don't spend time thinking through your if/then scenarios, then you will fall back on your automatic default setting. For some people, "flight" is the automatic response because choosing to "fight" means you will have a moment when you have to tolerate uncertainty. Choosing to fight means accepting the discomfort of anxiety as you develop your if/then scenarios. You can't get to "then" if you aren't willing to deal with the nerves that come when you think of "if". For example, if you are a cyclist, triathlete, runner, swimmer, etc. and immediately after someone passes you during a race your confidence drops and you lose your focus, you need to create a Plan B to address how you need to think and react in that situation to keep your composure and stick to your game plan. At then end of the chapter you will have an opportunity to work on your resilience by developing your own Plan B strategies.

You might remember from the chapter on goal setting that not preparing for obstacles is one of the pitfalls we fall into that prevents us from creating an effective goal plan. The Plan B tool at the end of this chapter will help you to examine the potential obstacles you may encounter and look at how you react in those situations and *how you want to react* in order to maintain your confidence and focus in that moment. You're starting the process of developing a new neural pathway by defining another option and then planting that seed in your mind. When that situation comes up and you try out your Plan B, that seed starts to grow roots and sprout. You're strengthening the pathway and the more you do that, eventually what was once a Plan B reaction will become Plan A. Planning your response makes it more likely that you will respond in a way that is beneficial to your performance.

Seizing Opportunities

When people talk about mental toughness, what they are often referring to is an athlete's resilience. An athlete's resilience indicates their ability to handle the stressors and challenges of training and competition. Adversity is inevitable when it comes to sports. Athletes that are mentally tough are able to maintain their confidence, motivation, and focus no matter what is going on around them. For some athletes, resilience seems to come more naturally. Their calm and self-assured demeanor allows them to observe, accept, and then react. For many of us, it feels like a skill we will never have, but resilience is a state of being that is formed by the foundation of your Mental Skills Training. Resilience isn't *a* skill; it's many skills. It's your ability to stay focused among distractions. It's your ability to squash feelings of doubt and *feed the athlete*. It's having a clear goal and strengthening your commitment to that goal. It's being able to face an obstacle and see an opportunity. These are the skills of resilience. You aren't born resilient, you work for it. Part of being resilient comes from planned behavior. It comes from thinking through the obstacles you may face and planning how you want to respond to those challenges.

The key to dealing with any obstacle is to accept and adjust. Sometimes this process is just a matter of time passing. Getting enough distance between you and the obstacle to shift your perspective. You can also be proactive about helping this process along by using the tools at the end of this chapter and practicing the tools throughout this book. Putting time into the mental part of your performance helps you build the necessary mental skills to be a resilient and mentally tough athlete that can go through the process of accepting and adjusting more quickly. The reality is that some setbacks are huge and will impact your life significantly, but as Natalie du Toit's story illustrates, how far it sets you back is up to you.

Competing in sports does not come without hardship. It does not come without disappointment, challenge, and sacrifice. The journey is full of adversity, which is part of what makes it a beautiful and worthwhile endeavor. When you accept that journey and everything that comes with it, you can even embrace the disappointment, challenge, and sacrifice. The struggle is a necessary part of the journey. The struggle is the precursor to improvement and growth. The struggle is the precursor to accomplishment and victory. When you can enjoy and respect all of the parts of your athletic journey, you don't see obstacles, you see opportunities.

Chapter 9: Take-Aways

- Obstacles are inevitable in sport and in life. Learn to embrace them as part of the journey.
- The language you use to describe a setback impacts how you feel, think, and react to the situation.
- Don't be victimized by your setbacks. Whether the obstacle is big or small, how far it sets you back is up to you.
- When people talk about mental toughness what they are referring to is an athlete's resiliency. Resilience isn't something you are born with; it's something you work for.
- Working on your Plan B helps you prepare for obstacles so you can see the opportunities.

Chapter 9: Tools

Tool: Incident Report

If you've ever worked in any type of job or healthcare facility where the organization is responsible in some way for the physical well being of the patients or participants, you may be familiar with the term "incident report." It's basically a form that is filled out when an "incident" occurs. It describes the situation and how it was dealt with so changes can be made in protocol to either prevent or more effectively handle that situation in the future. This tool walks you through your own *incident report* in order to reflect on a specific situation. You can use this reflective tool to process a difficult or challenging situation and then be able to move forward from the event and use what you've learned to inform your decisions and reactions in the future. Think about a specific situation that has occurred that you are concerned about. Grab a piece of paper or access the worksheet at www.carriecheadle.com and answer the following:

1. Describe the situation.
2. How did you address the situation?
3. How do you currently feel about the situation?
4. Do you have any fears/worries about the situation?
5. Where do you need to shift your focus in order to feel better about the situation?
6. If you were to encounter this situation again, what would you do differently?
7. What do you need to keep in mind for the future?
8. Other comments:

Tool: Plan B

Every athlete has certain situations that rattle his or her confidence. Working on your Plan B helps you to realize that there is more than one way to react to a situation. It also helps you think through your contingency plans for potential challenges you may encounter so you don't lengthen your reaction time in the moment by having to decide how you want to react. You already have your plan laid out for how to adapt and respond to the situation.

Step 1: Grab a piece of paper and divide it into three columns. Title the first column "Situation". In this column, write out a situation in which you would usually lose your focus or confidence.

Step 2: Title the next column "Reaction". In this column, write out how you usually react in that situation. Take a moment to see it in your mind and write down how you're feeling, what you're thinking, and how it impacts your performance.

Step 3: Title the final column "Plan B". In this column, write out how you would like to react in this situation. What do you need to do to adapt, to stay in the moment and keep your focus where it needs to be and keep your confidence intact? If you're having trouble with this column, think about an athlete you admire; an athlete you deem to be confident and resilient. Imagine how that athlete would react in that situation and start from there.

Step 4: Continue to fill out your Plan B for any other situations you can think of that might rattle your performance. You may not be able to control the situation, but you have absolute influence over how you react (or don't react) to it.

Step 5: Practice your Plan B. Think about how you can use this information moving forward. Pick one situation and set a goal to work on that. Read through your Plan B before your competition. Think about how you want to use this tool and then put that plan into practice.

chapter 10

PERFORMING TO YOUR POTENTIAL

*"The greatest waste in the world is the difference between what we are
and what we could ultimately be."*
—Martin Luther King Jr., Civil Rights Activist, American leader

B amboo is one of the fastest growing plants in the world. However,
with certain bamboo species, when you plant a seed in the ground
it can appear as though nothing is happening for months, even years.
You plant the seed, water the soil, and wait. Although it appears as if
nothing is happening the bamboo is creating its root system, laying
the foundation for what is to come. Once it does sprout, it skyrockets;
the bamboo plant you thought would never grow could grow up to
100 feet that year at a rate of 12 to 24 inches a day! Once the bamboo
plant it is full-grown, it is a plant of many uses. Unlike trees, you can
harvest from the same bamboo plant year after year. From food, to
musical instruments, to building materials, many amazing things are
created from that seed. Just like the bamboo seed, the tools you have
learned throughout this book need to be nurtured and will take time to

grow. Once you have cultivated these skills, you can continue to harvest them, rely on them, and draw strength from them for both your sport and your life.

Bringing it All Together

If you really want to improve your mental game — strengthen your mental fitness – you need to decide it's a priority and then dedicate the time to work on it. What you have read about in this book is what you need in order to perform more consistently, build more confidence, and have more control over your performance — *if you do the work*. It is the combined work that you do on all of these skills that creates a strong foundation for your mental game. The skills affect each other. They interact with one another. If you want to relieve some of the anxiety and pressure you are feeling and get back to enjoying your sport, it is your continued effort and the combination of these skills that will provide for you. It's just as important as all of the other factors that impact your performance. You wouldn't just hydrate once and then expect to be hydrated for the rest of the season. You wouldn't just do a month of strength training and expect to keep that strength for the rest of the year. Mental Skills Training isn't a one-time thing. Once you build these skills, your consistency with the practice of your mental game has just as great an impact on your performance as whether or not you are consistent with your physical practice. This book is a journey of who you are as an athlete and who you want to (and will) become. As the saying goes, the journey isn't over it is just beginning. The tools are here; what you do with the information in this book is up to you. Here are some highlights from each chapter to remind you of the importance of each mental skill:

Chapter 1: Performing Under Pressure

Your ability to perform under pressure is a major factor when it comes to competing in your sport. You have to accept that stress and anxiety are part of the package and that it's normal to feel nervous. Anxiety isn't "bad"; it's an emotion designed to get you to take action. The intensity of the anxiety you feel lets you know that you need to work on your physical and/or mental game in order to feel more prepared for the situation in front of you. It's also important to take some of the mystery out of these issues of stress and anxiety by understanding the biological and physiological roles that are involved. Understanding what causes you to experience a *stressor* as *stressful,* how both your brain and body can intensify or lessen the feelings of stress, can help you choose reactions that are more beneficial to your performance.

Chapter 2: Your Inner Drive

Your level of motivation affects every part of your performance from training to competition. Every choice you make stems from a motivation to move towards something or move away from something. If your motivation is low, you want to diagnose the cause so you can start working on the cure. If there's anything that compromises you feeling capable, in control, and connected, it will affect your level of motivation. It's easy to see that if you feel like you aren't skilled at your sport, feel powerless over your choice to compete, and don't feel a connection with the group or team you're with, you're not going to feel very motivated to continue. Even if you are only lacking in one of these areas, it can greatly affect your drive to participate. Knowing why you do what you do can help you recognize when something is missing. You need to always be connected to the part of you that would participate in your sport no matter who is watching or keeping score; connected to the part that drew you to your sport in the first place. That's the motivation that keeps you moving forward when you hit a roadblock on your goal path. That's the motivation that drives you to work on your mental game so you can perform to your potential and enjoy your sport.

Chapter 3: Choosing Your Destination

When you learn how to set effective goals, goal setting can help direct your energy and focus, enhance your motivation and confidence, and of course – improve your performance. Goal setting can also have the opposite effect when you dive headfirst into avoidable pitfalls and aren't aware of your *secret goals*. Whether deliberate or not, you are always setting goals and the goals that you set for yourself can either contribute to your feelings of confidence or contribute to your feelings of doubt. You gauge your feelings of competence and confidence based on how you're doing relative to the expectations and goals that you have. When you see that there is a discrepancy between where you want to be and where you are, it can be challenging to not feel like you just want to throw in the towel. If you want your goals to positively impact your performance, you need to make sure you are setting effective goals. You need to know both *where* you want to go and *how* you're going to get there. When you don't accomplish your goals, you aren't failing at your goals; you're failing at goal setting.

Chapter 4: Relaxing the Body

Tension, whether psychological or physiological, interferes with your ability to achieve optimal performance. Every athlete has their own optimal zone of physiological intensity at which they perform their best. For the most part, you don't just show up to competition and happen to be in your optimal zone. Sometimes you need to psych yourself up to get there, but if you're feeling nervous, it's more likely that you will need to bring yourself down. Experiencing performance anxiety interferes both physiologically and psychologically with your performance. The physiological impact of shallow breathing and muscular tension will affect your coordination, balance, and make you quicker to fatigue. The tools you learned about that help you to relax your body, (like diaphragmatic breathing, progressive relaxation, using music, and reframing your butterflies), are imperative for being able to reduce the negative physiological impact that can occur. If you've been living in a heightened state of stress and experiencing performance anxiety — your relaxation response is like an atrophied muscle. You need to strengthen that muscle so it is quicker to engage when you really need it.

Chapter 5: Relaxing the Mind

Facing a challenge can induce feelings of anxiety when you perceive that you are unable to meet the demand. That perception includes your thoughts — worries, doubts, and judgments — about your capacity to perform. Those thoughts, whether they are true or not, can trigger your stress response and activate an immediate physiological response that isn't necessarily beneficial to your performance. However, the problem is that your assessments aren't always accurate. You might be stuck in an old script of feeding the monster that has now become an automatic thought pattern. If those patterns are getting in the way of your performance it's time to re-evaluate your thoughts and perceptions and work on *feeding the athlete*. Your thoughts have a direct impact on your motivation going into competition, your focus and confidence while you're in it, and the story you tell when it's all said and done. For some people, feeding the monster is much easier than feeding the athlete and it takes deliberate work to choose thoughts that are more facilitative to your performance. You have to work on relaxing the body *and* relaxing the mind in order to start re-wiring your feelings of anxiety that elicit your stress response.

Chapter 6: Choosing Your Focus

Focus is an essential mental skill for successful athletic performance. Appropriate focus is needed to tune into the cues relevant to your performance. Internal and external distractions can interfere with where your focus needs to be in that moment, if you let them. It takes deliberate effort to focus on the things that are in your control and on the tasks that are relevant to your performance. It's important to recognize that distractions aren't pulling your focus away; you are pushing your focus toward those distractions. Where you choose to focus is also a factor in whether you feel confident and in control or experience feelings of anxiety and doubt. Knowing where you tend to push your focus can help you plan for how to choose your focus and keep yourself "tuned-in" to the things that are in your control. Understanding how your brain processes information, and having the tools to work on shifting your focus, can help keep your focus where it needs to be when it needs to be there.

Chapter 7: Preparation = Confidence

When you feel prepared to face the challenge in front of you, you will feel more confident in your ability to do so. When you have crossed all of the t's and dotted all the i's in your mental and physical preparation it sets you up for optimal competitive performance. Your event doesn't start when the gun goes off, but starts when you begin preparing for your event. The days and hours leading up to your performance are critical times that often get overlooked. The tools in Chapter Seven help you to feel confident in your preparation so you are more confident with your performance. Dialing in your Pre-Performance Plan helps get your mindset where it needs to be to feel confident and focused during those essential hours leading up to your event. When you make your preparation a priority you realize that confidence isn't something you are, it's something you do. If you want to perform consistently you need to prepare consistently.

Chapter 8: Reflection & Feedback

All learning and improvement comes from your ability to recognize and act on feedback. Working on your ability to seek out and take in feedback is imperative for improving your performance. Sometimes that feedback comes from external sources and sometimes it comes from your personal reflections on your performance. What you attribute your success and failure to impacts your feelings of confidence and motivation moving forward. It's important to be sure that your reflections are based on the facts and not just the emotions produced as a result of the outcome. If hearing the word "feedback" fills you with a sense of dread, you need to change your perception of feedback and equate it with progress and improvement versus errors and failure. Not only do you need to be proactive about your reflective practice and about seeking out feedback, but you also need to make sure that you are recognizing and acknowledging your efforts and accomplishments along the way.

Chapter 9: From Obstacles to Opportunities

Encountering setbacks will be a part of your athletic journey; therefore your ability to recover from setbacks is an essential mental skill. How you think about setbacks affects how you react to them. Your perceptions and the language you choose to define the obstacle in front of you impacts whether the obstacle is a platform to launch you to a new height or a wall you can't surmount. Thinking about alternative ways to view the obstacle can impact how you approach the situation. Additionally, taking the time to think through the potential obstacles you may encounter and how to address them can help you feel more confident in your ability to do just that. In the moment it occurs, it's often your fear that prevents you from seeing the options available to you. Your fear sends you straight to the worst-case scenario. However, if you've taken the time to define how you want to react in that situation, you're beginning the process of strengthening that pathway and opening the door to an opportunity. When you can understand and embrace the fact that the struggle is what allows you to grow, you can accept those setbacks as a valuable part of your journey.

Chapter 10: Performing to Your Potential

In this final chapter you will have the opportunity to contemplate three important factors for performing to your potential. They are essential elements that when added to the foundation of your Mental Skills Training, complete the whole athlete. In this chapter you will explore the idea of opening up your definition of success, take ownership over creating your support system, and re-learn how to just go out and play.

Defining Success

A great source of anxiety can come from feeling like it says something about you if you don't succeed. Your value and worth as a person has nothing to do with the outcome of your event or with being better than your competition. When you define success only within the parameters of whether or not you win or lose and that it *means* something about you personally if you don't succeed — you are signing up for a sporting life of misery. There's a difference between feeling angry, disappointed, and frustrated by a loss versus feeling like you are less of a person because of it. One of the greatest things you can do for yourself and your performance is to broaden the boundaries of how you define success.

Eric Moussambani is arguably one of the worst athletes ever to appear in an Olympic Games. "Eric the Eel" gained international fame after appearing in the 2000 Sydney Olympics on a wildcard. Before the 2000 Olympics he had never even *seen* a 50m pool. In fact, he had only learned how to swim eight months prior to his Olympic debut. Donning baggy blue swim shorts, he lined up with his competition, about to race a distance twice as far as he had ever swam in his life. As he swam the length of the pool, it was clear that Moussambani would not be the strongest swimmer of the games. At one point he struggled tremendously and it looked like he wouldn't make it, but the cheering from the crowd helped him to keep moving forward. He may not have been the fastest swimmer, but his achievement was great. He finished the event and brought the crowd to their feet and when he was interviewed after his race he replied, "I'm going to jump and dance all night long in celebration of my personal triumph!" The fact that he was even on the blocks demonstrates his incredible tenacity and courage. Glory doesn't just come to the winner. It also comes to the competitor that shows up and gives everything they have to give on that day.

Part of enjoying your sport and letting go of the pressure you put on yourself is finding a way to enjoy the journey. If competition were just about the outcome, people wouldn't stick around for very long. In the moment of competition, you temporarily forget that success is defined by a lot more than whether you win or lose, whether you get a personal record that day or have the worst race of your life. The fact is, you're going to have all of those experiences and as you know, the outcome of the day only tells one small part of the story. When you only judge your success based on the outcome of your performance it can cause you to feel increased pressure to perform, which leads to anxiety. Here are some other ways to gauge what it means to be successful:

Resilience

Were you able to overcome challenges? Did you make a mistake and mentally turn it around? Was the competition harder than you expected and you stayed in it? Were you able to adjust your goal in the moment and feel good about the adjustment? Were you able to exercise some emotional control at a critical moment? Did you seize an opportunity and take a risk even if it didn't pan out? Did you push yourself out of your comfort zone? Resilience is one of the most underrated and most valuable mental skills. The questions above are just a snapshot of the ways you can measure resilience. Your resilience in the face of a setback is an accomplishment that needs to be recognized.

Opportunity

Sometimes a major shift in perspective can help you relax and enjoy the moment. Not everyone can say that they have had the opportunity to be where you are and do what you're doing. Sometimes that perspective can come from knowing that your body is physically capable and healthy enough to train and perform when others can't. Or it may come from the fact that you get to travel around the country or the world as an elite or professional athlete knowing that somewhere in that same moment there is a kid that is dreaming the dream that you are living out. Sometimes success comes from the fact that you get the opportunity to participate. Remembering what you have versus what you don't can be a great catalyst for shifting your perspective and feeling good about where you are.

Team-player

Did you pick someone up when they needed it? Did you give your team-mate constructive feedback even though you knew it would be hard to hear? Did you willingly sacrifice your personal goals for the team goals? When you are part of a team, contributing to your team's success is your triumph as well. When you are truly a part of a team, what you give to your team needs to be a factor in gauging your individual success as well. If you play a team sport you need to consider your team when evaluating your performance. Understanding how you personally contributed to a team triumph needs to be accounted for when defining success.

Goal-fulfillment

Regardless of the outcome, did you work towards your personal goals? As you know, an outcome goal is just one type of goal you can set for your performance. You can also gauge your success by asking yourself whether you moved a step closer towards your goals. If you did, you need to give yourself a pat on the back. If one of your goals for competition was to take a risk because you've been holding yourself back out of your fear of failing, it's easy to say "Yeah, but..." You need to take out the "but". Instead of "Yeah, I really went for it, but it didn't go over very well," you say "Yeah, I really went for it and I'm proud of myself for taking the risk." Don't withhold recognizing your efforts based on someone else's criteria for success. In this example, taking the risk is a HUGE success and deserves to be recognized as one.

Big Picture

Take a moment to think about and answer this question: am I better than when I first started this athletic journey? Right now just think about your level of play and then think about your physical and mental capabilities when you first started. When you are continually trying to improve your game you can get trapped into thinking that you are never good enough. Additionally, when you are only gauging your success based on your most recent performance or on one bad game, you are not including the whole picture. One bad song doesn't mean that the whole album is bad and the band sucks. Be sure to step back every once in a while and get a good look at the big picture.

Opening up your definition of what it means to be successful doesn't mean that you don't want to be competitive or to win. Of course you do! Your sport sets the stage for you to fulfill that competitive drive, but it's *more* than just winning. Winning is just the outcome, it's *how winning makes you feel* that is what you are actually striving for. However, if you have been battling performance anxiety, instead of striving for the feelings that come with winning, you are running from the feelings that come with your perceived failure. For every component that makes up being on top of your game, you have to accept its counterpart as well. For every time you feel unbelievably driven and excited about your sport, there will be a time when you don't want anyone to even mention the word. For every time you push yourself passed what you thought was possible and accomplish a goal, there will be a time when you encounter a major obstacle and have to readjust. For every time you perform flawlessly under pressure, there will be a time when you crumble.

Part of feeling successful comes from picking yourself back up. It comes from witnessing your growth and improvement. It can be incredibly satisfying and fill you with a sense of pride to reach a new height. The thing you must come to accept is that any time you are pushing against your boundaries, whether it's the boundary of your skill or the boundary of your self-concept, in the moment that it's stretching, it feels scary and uncomfortable. Growth and improvement won't come without some growing pains. You feel anxiety because you are pushing passed the comforting walls into new unknown territory.

Building Your Support System

A necessary component of having the energy, confidence, and courage to forge into those growing pains is to have some help and encouragement along the way. No one performs to their potential without a fantastic support system surrounding them. Athletes that are able to perform to their potential have a strong and capable network of people around them that fulfill multiple roles of support. That support can help you stay grounded or help give you a little push. They can also provide you with a little padding for when you do fall and then provide a place to bounce from when you need to jump back in. However, when it comes to the idea of support there is a great misconception that everyone in your life that is important to you should know exactly what kind of support you need and be able to offer it at the exact time that you need it. In an ideal world, this would work out incredibly well. However, we are much more complicated creatures than that. It's unrealistic to expect others to always know when you need support and give you the kind of support that you need. What complicates matters further is that sometimes you don't even know what kind of support you need. When it comes to optimal performance and accomplishing your athletic goals, there are three essential types of support. At any given point in time you may need physical, informational, or motivational support — and most of the time you will need all three.

Sometimes the type of support you need is *physical* support. You might need someone to get you access to equipment if you want to get in some extra practice. You might need someone to watch your kids or find a gym with daycare so you can get your training in. These are examples of actual concrete support you might need in order to accomplish your goals. Other times you might need *informational* support. This type of support may come in the form of feedback or instructions from a coach or teammate. You might seek out the services of an expert in strength conditioning, nutrition, mental skills training, or a physical therapist to provide information in their area of expertise on optimal performance. Then there will be times when you need some *motivational* support. Someone to say, "I know you can do this" when you are struggling or someone to work out with to help pick you up when you're dragging your feet. Motivational support can also come in to form of having someone who will listen when you just need to vent and get things off your chest so you can process and move on.

When you need and expect a certain type of support from someone and you don't get it, it can be very frustrating. You often expect that an important person in your life should be able to fulfill all of the types of support whenever you need them to. Sometimes the greatest frustration comes when the type of support you need is not matching up with the type of support that's being given. An athlete struggling with learning a new skill may only be getting informational support from their coach when what she really needs in that moment is some motivational support. An athlete might be seeking out informational support from family and friends when they only know how to give physical or motivational support. The last thing you want is for someone to say, "You can do it!" when what you really need is someone to explain to you *how* to do it. Here are some essential truths to know when it comes to getting support:

- Just because someone doesn't offer support doesn't mean that they don't want to support you.

- It is unrealistic and unfair to expect one person to fulfill all of these roles; you will have many people on your support team.
- You have to know what kind of support you need.
- You have to ask for the support that you need.

The type of support that you need in that moment is not always going to be obvious to the person standing across from you. Oftentimes people are supporting you with the kind of support they would want in that moment. They may also be trying to fulfill the role that they think they should be filling, or it might be the only type of support they know how to give. We all need support. If you feel like you aren't getting the support that you need, it's time to build up your support system. You need to assess what type of support you need and then you need to be willing to go out and ask for that support. If you are getting one type of support from someone important in your life and you need a different type of support you need to let him or her know what type of support you need. Additionally, instead of just relying on one source of support, there can be different people in those supporting roles that can help provide all of the types of support you need in order to perform to your potential. At the end of this chapter you will have the opportunity to start thinking about what kind of support you need and who can provide it for you. Having that support helps you to feel grounded and provides you with the boldness to rise up and meet challenges and push yourself to your potential.

It's Time to Go Out and Play

In our culture of achievement everything is taken seriously. Sports are no longer a place to engage with others and challenge oneself; they are a place to prove oneself and a means for making it to college or making big money. When you are able to *play* your sport, you are open to receiving cues from your surrounding environment versus fighting against them. You are relaxed and free of the mental tension that impedes creativity and free of the physiological tension that impedes physical performance. When you are *playing* your sport you are enjoying the moment and allowing yourself to be open to the experience. You are free from judgments and expectations. When you're "working" your sport you're trying to force things and judging your efforts and the outcome. In order to perform to your potential, you have to free yourself from these pressures and get back to *playing* the game.

I have this vivid memory from early in my career while I was out watching a bike race. I was watching a circuit race on a course that has an infamous climb in it. I was standing at the bottom of the climb and as I watched the pack go by and start to disappear around the corner there were two cyclists off the back of the pack that were just starting the climb. As they began their ascent, the cyclist on the right turned and looked to his teammate on his left and said, "Remind me why we do this again?" and they both immediately broke out into huge smiles and then looked straight ahead and made their way up the climb. I love this memory. Every time I think of it I feel the exact same way I did when I witnessed the exchange in that moment. I get filled with this incredible sense of joy and satisfaction thinking about those two cyclists absorbed in the moment, pushing themselves to their limit, and demonstrating that they would rather be right there on that climb and competing in the sport they love than doing anything else in the world. They were working hard, but they were *playing*.

Humans are simultaneously wired to thrive and survive and although most of the time the two elements work in tandem, sometimes they get in each other's way. When you are thriving, you have an inherent desire to learn and grow. You are open to the situation you are experiencing and adapt and change in order to thrive. In order to capitalize on learning you have to be free from stress. When you get away from *playing* your sport and put pressure on yourself to perform, you create stress, which impedes your physical performance and interferes with your ability to improve by interfering with your ability to learn. When you are surviving, you have an inherent desire to protect and be cautious in order to survive. When you get into the sports arena, during times when you are meant to thrive, something triggers you into survival mode and makes you reactive instead of proactive. Knowing that anxiety is a protective emotion and that as a human you are designed to reduce your feelings of anxiety can help you normalize what you are feeling.

If you want to perform to your potential and enjoy yourself along the way, you need to have and use the tools available to you to handle the pressure. When you've decided you can't handle the pressure, that's when the resulting psychological and physiological symptoms can potentially have a negative impact on your performance. It's important to remember that athletes that thrive under pressure have worked on that skill – which is actually a skill made up of ALL of the mental skills you've read about in this book. You don't want to eliminate your feelings of anxiety. Not only is it unrealistic to think you can, but you wouldn't want to. Instead of feeling like you need to eliminate it, you can understand why it exists and understand how to accept it as part of the human experience, part of your athletic journey.

Participating in sport is meant to add value to your life. It calls upon you to challenge yourself and to challenge others. It sets the stage for you to experience both your greatest heartbreaks and greatest victories. Sport is meant to add joy to your life. Joy in playing something that you love and are passionate about. Sport is meant to add pride to your life. You experience a sense of pride when you feel competent and see your improvement. You feel proud that you have pursued the challenge and overcome what you once thought was insurmountable. There is no way to experience the physicality of sport without the psychology of it. They are inextricably intertwined and create the whole of the experience, body and mind. In order to get these things out of your sport you have to train your body and your mind. Whether you are a recreational or elite athlete, your athletic career can provide an environment that teaches you valuable life lessons. It can shape who you are both inside and outside of your sport. It can be the most amazing journey if you can stay in the game and accept all that comes with it.

This is your journey, no one else's.

Chapter 10: Take-Aways

- Working on your mental game is just as important as working on your physical game. Your dedication and consistency of working on your mental skills has as great an impact as your dedication and consistency of working on your physical skills.
- Defining success encompasses more than the outcome of your performance. Be sure to include all of these means for gauging your success.
- Having support is essential for accomplishing your goals. Take responsibility for building your support system and asking for the support you need.

- Getting back to playing your sport removes the mental and physical tension that creates interference and impedes your performance.
- Accept the yin and yang of your athletic journey. Accept that for every up there is a down and your continued effort on your mental game ensures that there will be an up again.

Chapter 10: Tools

Tool: Building Support

What kind of support do you need in order to accomplish your goals? Building your support system is a proactive process. You have to figure out what kind of support you need and then you have to be willing to ask for that support. There are three types of support needed when it comes to optimal performance for athletes. For each category of support, you will figure out WHAT kind of support you need in that category and WHERE you can get that support.

Step 1: Grab a piece of paper and start with the support category "Physical". *Physical Support* is actual assistance that you need in order to reach your goals and perform to your potential. Examples of this type of support are: rides to games, people to help you with your equipment, a place to train, etc. Brainstorm what kind of support you need that fits into this category. Once you have completed the WHAT, move onto the WHERE and brainstorm how you can get the support you need. What resources are available? Who could provide the kind of support you need for that category? Who are your potential support buddies?

Step 2: The next category is "Informational". An example of *Informational Support* is a resource or a person that can provide essential information or advice to help answer your questions and advance your performance goals. Brainstorm WHAT kind of *Informational Support* you need and WHERE you can get that support.

Step 3: The final category is "Motivational". Examples of *Motivational Support* are reassurance and encouragement, as well as expressions of concern and showing empathy. They are your own personal "cheerleaders" that believe in you and support you while you are on your path to your goals, celebrate your accomplishments, or listen when you are frustrated with your performance. Brainstorm WHAT kind of *Motivational Support* you need and WHERE you can get that support.

Step 4: Assess and take action. You may have noticed that there are some categories that are doing fine and some that need a little work. Choose one of the categories to work on and start seeking out the support you need. Use the principles from Chapter Three and set a goal. You have the tool, now it's up to you to take control and make it happen.

Tool: Mental Skills Checklist

You can use this checklist as a guide to put all of the pieces together in your mental game as your approach your event or your competition. This list is just a starting point. You may find that you want to make some changes and create your own personal checklist based on what works for you.

_____ Choose inspirational quotes
_____ Choose pre-performance music
_____ Set your outcome goal and process goals

____ Assess your "secret goal" and adjust goals if needed
____ Visualize past peak performance scenarios
____ Write out your sport affirmations
____ Fill out your critical moments worksheet
____ Write out your Plan B scenarios
____ Write out your Pre-Performance Plan
____ Visualize performing to your potential and accomplishing your outcome and process goals
____ Fill out your Post Competition Evaluation

The more consistent you are with your mental preparation, the more natural it will become. Don't feel like you have to tackle the whole list right away. Pay attention to what is attractive to you and start putting your energy there. Or think about what you need help with the most right now and choose to focus on the tool that would have the most impact. Eventually, with consistent effort and practice, going through your mental skills checklist will feel as normal as going through your pre-game warm-up. You may not need to do all of them all of the time, but you need to be *willing* to do them all if you want to be on top of your game.

NOTES

Chapter 1

[1]Sapolsky, Robert, M. *Why Zebras Don't Get Ulcers: The Acclaimed Guide to Stress, Stress-Related Diseases, and Coping.* 3rd ed. New York: Henry Holt and Company, LLC, 2004. Print.

Chapter 6

[2]Goleman, Daniel. *Emotional Intelligence: Why It Can Matter More Than IQ.* 10th ed. New York: Bantam Books, 2005. Print.

[3]Stephen, Bull, J., John G. Albinson, and Christopher J. Shambrook. *The Mental Game Plan: Getting Psyched for Sport.* 1996. Cheltenham: Sports Dynamics, 2002. Print.

Chapter 8

[4]Gallwey, Timothy, W., and Robert Kriegel. *Inner Skiing.* Revised ed. New York: Random House, 1997. Print.

ACKNOWLEDGEMENTS

I have so many people to thank for their supporting roles in helping me to accomplish my goal of writing this book. Thank you forever and always — to all of my family and friends for the continued love and support. Thanks to the members of the CCSP for the food, wine, laughter, friendship, clarity, and guidance. Thanks to my husband Chad who has read almost every word I have ever written and been witness to the challenges and triumphs of my career path. Thanks to my friend Stacie Sather who edited my first draft and helped me sound grammatically smarter than I actually am. Thanks to my second editor Jill Rothenberg whose editorial wisdom and invaluable feedback I used to refine the final version of this book. After years of feeling unphotogenic, thank you to Liz Foote for finally capturing a picture of me that I'm not embarrassed to use for my headshot! Thank you to all of the athletes I have worked with that put their trust in me and taught me so much. Thanks to my Mom who catered to my secret fears and kept a fourth back up copy of my book as it was in progress. And thank you to absolutely everyone that read chapters, gave opinions, and encouraged me throughout this whole incredible process.

To ALL of my family, friends, co-workers, classmates, students, athletes, and acquaintances: to all of you that had a hand in shaping the person I am today, which is the person that was able to accomplish this goal:

"I can no other answer make, but, thanks, and thanks." ~William Shakespeare

ABOUT THE AUTHOR

Carrie Cheadle is a Mental Skills Coach and a Certified Consultant through the Association for Applied Sport Psychology (CC-AASP). She lives in Petaluma, California and has been working on peak performance with teams, organizations, and individual athletes since 2002. Carrie received her Bachelor of Arts degree in psychology at Sonoma State University and her Master of Arts degree in sport psychology at John. F. Kennedy University.

Carrie works with athletes at every level, from recreational athletes to elite and professional athletes competing at national and international levels. She works with athletes and teams in many different sports and specializes in working with cyclists and endurance athletes. She also specializes in working with athletes and exercisers with Type 1 diabetes and is the Director of the Mental Skills Training Program for Diabetes Training Camp.

Carrie has been interviewed as an expert resource for articles that have appeared in VeloNews, Outside Magazine, Bicycling Magazine, Sporting Kid, Snowboard Canada, Men's Fitness, and Women's Health. Carrie's personal athletic journey, from sitting on the start line of a car race, to standing at the top of a double-black diamond run, to returning to sports after multiple injuries have all led her to recognize the tremendous impact psychology has on physical performance. Carrie has her own personal commitment to life-long fitness and when she isn't working with athletes, you might find her running on a trail or hitting the slopes on her snowboard.

For more information about Carrie and Mental Skills Training, please visit:

Website: www.carriecheadle.com

FaceBook: MentalSkillsTrainingforAthletes

Twitter: @feedtheathlete